Mindemic

How faith can help us overcome
the anxiety and depression
crisis in America

JEFF WOLF

FOREWORD BY HAROLD G. KOENIG, M.D.

FREILING

PUBLISHING

Published by Freiling Publishing, a division of Freiling Agency, LLC.

P.O. Box 1264
Warrenton, VA 20188

www.freilingpublishing.com

ISBN: 978-1-950948-75-8

Dedicated to my son, Seth Ryan.

Since the day you were born, you have been the apple of my eye. I will always be your strongest defender and your biggest fan.

I love you.

Contents

Foreword

BY HAROLD G. KOENIG, M.D.

I n *Mindemic: How faith can help us overcome the anxiety and depression crisis in America*, Jeff Wolf takes us on a journey that many have hoped was possible but wondered whether it was possible for them. It is possible. Life is difficult. Life has always been difficult. Some manage to make it through relatively unscathed, but there are also many who suffer wounds from this battle. In most cases, those wounds have been emotional and mental, manifested by symptoms of fear, anxiety, depression, hopelessness, and a lack of meaning and purpose in life.

In this beautifully written investigatory work, Jeff examines scientific, psychological, and theological evidence to provide answers to some very difficult questions—questions that many have avoided. But the answers that he has found indeed can give us hope and begin to show us how to manage "the slings and arrows of outrageous fortune." These answers lie in family, faith, and friends. Especially faith. Faith is what holds it all together. Jeff recognizes that and makes a solid case for healing.

It is with the greatest pleasure that I recommend this book. It is a must-read for those who are searching for a better life, a happier life, a fuller life, a more complete life, a life where struggle and pain are not wasted but turned into purpose. Really, that's everyone. Take a chance. Reading this book might be one of the best decisions that you ever make.

Harold G. Koenig, M.D.

Professor of Psychiatry & Behavioral Sciences

Associate Professor of Medicine

Director, Center for Spirituality, Theology and Health

Duke University Medical Center, Durham, North Carolina

Adjunct Professor, Dept. of Medicine, King Abdulaziz University, Jeddah, Saudi Arabia

Adjunct Professor of Public Health, Ningxia Medical University, Yinchuan, P.R. China

Visiting Professor, Shiraz University of Medical Sciences, Shiraz, Iran

CHAPTER 1

The Crisis

Min·dem·ic /mīn'demik/

Noun

A pandemic of worry, stress, fear, anxiety, depression, and other intangible pain that affects four in ten Americans.

S eth was nineteen years old when he loaded up his car to drive home to the Buckeye State from a college town in eastern Tennessee. He was eager to see his parents and to welcome his first nephew into the family; his big sister was scheduled to have her labor induced the following day.

Seth was like any normal teenager: He was handsome, bright, charismatic, and talented. He loved to play the piano and write songs, hang out with his friends, and play the latest video games. He was raised by loving, God-fearing parents and possessed a strong foundation of ethics, morals, and faith. Seth had endless possibilities in his future.

Everyone loved this energetic young man. His dad would always chuckle when he remembered his son trick-or-treating as a child and how someone at every house would answer the door and say, "Hi, Seth!" He knew no stranger, and everyone in the neighborhood knew him. He was like Dennis the Menace, without the "menace" part. As he grew, attended school, and played sports, he always enjoyed an abundance of friends. From the outside, he appeared to be an all-American young man who loved life. You would never know by looking at him that Seth struggled with debilitating anxiety.

When he arrived home after his 350-mile drive up Interstate 75, Seth hadn't slept for several nights, he was surviving on short naps when he was able to get them. It wasn't because he didn't want to sleep but because his anxiety was always worse at night, leaving him unable to sleep. It had been growing worse in the previous few months.

After settling in and visiting for a while, Seth's family all turned in for the night. They would have a suspenseful few days ahead of them as they awaited the arrival of their little bundle of joy. Seth, however, knew that sleep would evade him. He held it together for a couple of hours before it got the best of him, and he finally woke up his dad.

Through tired, glazed eyes, Seth's dad watched his son pace the floor crying, explaining how his last several nights had gone. Wiping tears, he said, "I'm tired of feeling this way." His dad knew of his struggle with anxiety. Seth had dealt with it since he was a child and would get an upset stomach when he became nervous. But he had no idea it had become so severe that Seth was going days without sleep. This was a new development and it was deeply concerning. His dad wanted to cry with him.

With great compassion, Seth's dad stayed up with him for a couple of hours, unrelentingly attempting to encourage him as a means of countering the anxiety. He had to do something. After a while, it seemed like Seth began to calm down and he was able to sit down next to his dad on the couch. As they talked, his dad put his arms around him and reassured him that everything was going to be alright and, in a moment of illumination, Seth said, "Dad, in my brain, I believe everything is fine. I'm safe, I'm loved, and there's absolutely nothing to worry about. My anxiety doesn't have anything to do with what I believe."

Admitting that he didn't have a frame of reference for this severe anxiety, Seth's dad asked him to describe what it felt like. He said, "You know that feeling you get in your chest when you get bad news and your heart just sinks? It feels like that, only it doesn't go away." That was a feeling his dad could relate to, and it clicked for the first time.

Unfortunately, Seth's battle is not unusual. There are millions of people of all ages, all walks of life, and from every corner of the globe that have the same daily struggle to some degree or another. In fact, according to a study conducted in 2017 by the Institute for Health Metrics and Evaluation, 284 million people around the world suffer from anxiety.[1]

Anxiety symptoms fall into three categories: *apprehension, motor tension,* and *autonomic overactivity. Apprehension* includes a feeling of impending doom, being "on edge," and having difficulty concentrating. *Motor tension* includes tension headaches, restlessness, trembling, and being unable to relax. *Autonomic overactivity* includes dizziness, sweating, and sometimes having an irregular heartbeat.[2]

Depression, although similar, is the second most prevalent psychological disorder globally, affecting 264 million people.[3] Depression, sometimes referred to as the "common cold" of psychiatry,[4] is believed to be triggered by factors such as anxiety, loss, rejection, betrayal, abuse, failure, family dysfunction, chronic illness, and others, yet "like a sudden forest fire with no traceable origin, depression [can] often [flare] up for no apparent reason" at all.[5] It is a leading cause of disability globally[6] and the number one cause of disability in people ages 15-44 in the United States.[7]

Depression is such a large and rapidly growing problem that its global economic burden is estimated to be $210.5 billion every year. (This includes co-morbid conditions that account for 38% of the cost).[8] Examples of this burden would be healthcare costs and costs to employers for disability or sick time.

The implications of these facts upon pharmaceuticals are staggering. The latest numbers from the Institute for Safe Medication Practices suggest that 1 in 6 Americans take antidepressants.[9] The global market for antidepressants was expected to reach $28.6 billion in 2020,[10] surpassing opioids at $18.5 billion,[11] making them the second most prescribed drug class in America.[12]

The Fear Factor

On March 11, 2020, the crisis multiplied when the World Health Organization declared COVID-19 a pandemic. Millions of people would contract the virus globally with a 2.2% death rate. At that time no one knew the extent to which the pandemic would affect our daily lives—or our futures. Perhaps we all assumed that it would come and go with little effect on our economy or mental health, but that would not be the case.

Bombarded by information from the 24-hour news cycle, fear and panic began to spread. Americans raced to retailers to purchase supplies. They filled up their gas tanks, hoarded water and toilet paper, and begin to prepare for a disaster of apocalyptic proportions. The information that didn't come from cable news came from social media. In the age where anyone with a mobile device can instantly spread information around the globe, fiction spread faster than truth.

We were confronted with so-called experts who couldn't agree on the details—medically, psychologically, or socially. We were confronted with certain economic disaster and what would become a serious threat to our freedoms—religious and otherwise. Businesses began to close, lock downs were mandated, jobs were lost, and for the first time in my lifetime, Americans were isolated.

Fear turned into anxiety. Symptoms of anxiety and depression skyrocketed from 11% of Americans in 2019 to 41% of Americans in 2020. Four in ten people said that they experienced symptoms of anxiety and depression due to worry and stress related to COVID-19.[13]

In April of 2020, unemployment in the United States peaked at 14.8%. It has been shown that joblessness is connected to an increase in anxiety, depression, low self-esteem and may contribute to an increase in substance abuse and suicide.[14] It would seem this was one of the most devastating blows to mental health.

Americans and people of nations around the world were suddenly paralyzed with fear: fear of contracting the virus, fear of dying from the virus, fear of elderly loved ones falling victim to the virus, and fear of losing their jobs, their life savings, their homes, and everything they worked for. We became afraid of everything: fear of leaving our houses, fear of going to church, fear of gathering with family, and fear of celebrating holidays. Fear became the pandemic.[15]

The difference between fear and anxiety is that fear is a primal involuntary reaction to a known threat. Anxiety is a response to uncertainty. The steady montage of information, true and not, gave rise to a national culture of uncertainty.[16] That uncertainty turned fear of a known threat into anxiety about an uncertain future. Americans could see no way of escape.

As of the date of this writing, global COVID-19 cases have reached over 128 million.[17] In comparison, that still doesn't amount to half of anxiety or depression cases. Think about that. What is the real pandemic?

Whether you have a loved one with a deadly virus or you are like Seth's dad watching him battle crippling anxiety, the weight of this crisis is heavy and the cost is much. It's much more than the cost of treatment or medication. For some, it costs their dreams, plans, happiness, and most importantly, their peace. Unfortunately, it has even cost some their lives. This is a global pandemic of the mind. It is a *mindemic*.

The Case for Healing

Do you struggle with anxiety or depression? Then you know it's something you carry with you every day. Whenever you leave home, it goes with you: to work, to school, to church, shopping, or on vacation. Anxiety and depression don't take weekends or holidays off. They don't sleep; they don't relent. They become the lens through which you view every part of your life. When your anxiety or depression begin to dictate where you go, how long you stay, and whom you are with, then you don't have *it*. It has *you*.

I'm Seth's dad. I've watched him battle anxiety since he was a boy. Whether it was making a necessary trip to the doctor's office, taking a test at school, or even for no apparent reason at all, he would become nervous to the point of physical sickness. In later years he was diagnosed with Attention Deficit Hyperactivity Disorder (ADHD), and his anxiety developed into a difficulty to cope with normal life events, sleeplessness, restlessness, headaches, and other issues. He has been treated with counseling and multiple medications through the years. Sometimes it worked; sometimes it didn't. I must admit, it has been difficult as a father to feel like I could personally do nothing for my son. I'm a fixer but I couldn't fix this. It has been heart-wrenching.

My experience with Seth's anxiety, on that night he came home, led me on a *new* quest to discover the root of the problem and find a way to actively help my son. Given how much it was now affecting him, I was embarrassed that I knew so little about such a huge problem, especially when it existed in my own home. As a man of faith, I refused to accept that this would define him and that there was no prognosis for healing. I refused to continue to accept the label that he had been given. This was no way for Seth, or anyone, to live. There had to be a solution, and I was determined to find it.

I am not a scientist, philosopher, physician, or licensed clinical counselor. But as a retired police sergeant, I know how to conduct an investigation. In my career, I have investigated or contributed to investigations into homicides, robberies, burglaries, felonious assaults, and other violent crimes. I decided to approach my search for answers as I would any investigation: examining evidence, making reasonable deductions, developing theories, and eventually coming to a conclusion.

This book is about making a case for healing. Are you one of the hundreds of millions of people around the world that are suffering from this crisis? Have you forfeited plans for the future, dreams of success, and hopes of happiness because of your anxiety and depression? Have you reduced yourself to simply trying to get through one day at a time? Have you isolated yourself from those who love you? Have you been paralyzed by fear and allowed yourself to be locked away in the prison of your mind? Has it affected your family, your career, your social life, or even your physical health? Have you lost your drive, your purpose, or your passion? Have you contemplated or attempted suicide?

If you answered yes to *any* of those questions, you are not alone, but you *are* in danger. This mindemic, at its very worst, can lead to suicide, which claims 800,000 lives every year.[18] The greatest tragedy is that these casualties are preventable. Suicide is the result of believing a lie that all hope is lost. I pray this book will restore your hope.

If you or a loved one have been struggling with chronic stress, anxiety, depression, or any other form of emotional pain, you don't have to buy into the lies of that pain. You don't have to be what your pain says you are. You don't have to be limited by what your pain says is impossible. Healing is within reach for those who are willing to embrace the process. You can shed the dark glasses that have jaded your perspective. You can break free from the negativity that has placed a lid on your relationships and opportunities. You can be happy, fulfilled, and at peace.

Journey with me to find answers to some tough questions. From philosophy to mental health science to the New Testament miracles of Jesus, you will learn how God made you—body, mind, and spirit—operating together in a beautifully synchronized orchestra. You will learn why healing is a cooperation of beliefs, behaviors, divine intervention, and sometimes medical intervention. You will learn how to come out from under the stigma of your struggle and turn your pain into purpose.

Prepare to be shocked by what I discovered.

CHAPTER 2

Fact Finding

T he first step in any investigation is to educate yourself about pertinent issues. I needed to learn as much as I could about this mindemic. When I began to drill down into the core of the subject, I had no idea it would initially raise more questions than answers. I found myself having to confront several unknowns: What causes anxiety and depression? Where does the problem exist? Is it a mental illness? Will medication solve the problem? Is there a cure?

Scouring medical journals, books, articles, and other literature for research on the subject led me down a rabbit hole of endless information published from various disciplines of study. As it turns out, four out of five of those questions spark a lot of debate, depending on whether the source is scientific, philosophical, theological, etc. Each discipline has its own bent and bias on the subject.

It startled me to realize that I would even have to confront my own belief system to find the answers I was looking for. As you follow this thought with me, you may also find yourself backed into a corner, having to decide where you stand on some of the issues.

Where Does It Hurt?

I had been having trouble with my right knee for more than a year. Being a typical male, visiting doctors is one of my least favorite activities. I would rather self-diagnose and go over-the-counter whenever possible. The obvious answer to my knee discomfort was age—and maybe that fall I took about the time it started hurting.

My loving and compassionate wife got weary of my complaints about said knee and convinced me to see an orthopedic doctor. On the day of the appointment, he came into the exam room, introduced himself, and asked me what brought me in. After I explained what was happening, he began to manipulate my right knee and asked, "Where is the pain?" "Does it hurt when I press here?" "Does it hurt when you move this way?" In short order, the doctor had found the exact source of my pain and explained to me what was causing it, complete with illustrations. Luckily it was not serious, but a common problem in about 50% of the population called Synovial Plica Syndrome.[19] It's easily treatable and usually doesn't require surgery. I was in and out in a matter of minutes. It was painless; almost.

The problem with issues like anxiety, depression, and what we will call "intangible pain" is that there is no place on your body to which you can point and say, "That's where it hurts." If you don't know where the pain lives, how do you go about getting treatment? As I began to delve into the question of "where does it hurt," I encountered a deeper question. It is called the "hard problem" or the "mind-body problem."

The hard problem is a discussion about human consciousness: where your imagination, perception, thinking, intelligence, judgment, language, memory, emotion, and instinct reside.[20] American geneticist Dean Hammer calls consciousness the "greatest hat trick of biology" because its origin, existence, and function are elusive to research.[21] The million-dollar question for scientists is: How does consciousness arise out of brain matter?[22] British philosopher Dr. Simon Blackburn said, "The hard problem is trying to convince ourselves that there is no hard problem."[23] Nevertheless, the question remains unanswered.

There are two main schools of thought that attempt to nail down human consciousness. The first is *dualism*. It contends that mind and matter are not the same. Our brain is separate from our consciousness or "mind." Another way to say it would be that we are both body and mind, and human consciousness lives in the mind, apart from the brain.[24] There is certainly sufficient evidence to support dualism.

I saw an interview with Dr. Sam Parnia, Associate Professor of Medicine at NYU. He is known for his research with cardiac patients who have near-death experiences. He said that in the event of cardiac arrest, the brain switches off, but there is evidence that consciousness does not. He goes on to explain that millions of people have been resuscitated from cardiac arrest, and later accurately recalled events happening around them such as something a doctor or nurse said during the period of time in which their brain was switched off.[25] His research certainly supports the dualist view that the brain and mind are separate entities.

Physicalism (also called materialism) holds to the view that we are body only, and human consciousness is a function of the brain.[26] Marvin Minsky of MIT wrote an article entitled, "Why People Think Computers Can't," discussing the possibility of consciousness in artificial intelligence. He described the brain as just "a computer made of meat"[27] by which consciousness is produced.

The problem with physicalism is that there is too much evidence that human consciousness functions independently of the brain (such as Dr. Parnia's research). Philosophers and scientists are now conceding that human consciousness cannot be explained by the laws of physics or chemistry. They further grant that they cannot explain how the brain might create consciousness.[28] The fact is that no one knows how exactly consciousness works.[29]

Why is this so important to our investigation into depression and anxiety? Because finding solutions requires us to first choose sides in the mind-body dilemma. If physicalists are correct, then the pain may live in the brain. If dualists are correct, then the pain lives in a non-material place in human consciousness. The brain—the organ in our skulls—can be treated by medical science. But how do we treat human consciousness (i.e., the mind)?

Dr. Carolyn Leaf pointed out that the philosophy of mental health care has become neuroreductionistic, meaning that our physical brains are blamed for everything and our life experiences are omitted from the equation. She asserts this approach doesn't work.[30] Dr. Leaf adds that the mind changes the brain,[31] giving credence to my developing theory that the two are not one and the same.

Am I Mentally Ill?

Anxiety and depression encompass many other specific disorders and are classified as mental illnesses or psychological disorders. Does that mean if I'm in a depressed mood that I have a mental illness? Does it mean if I'm dealing with anxiety about a specific problem in my life that I'm suffering from a psychological disorder? Obviously not. If that were true then we would all be considered mentally ill. A sad mood or incidental anxiety is normal; the problem arises when they become chronic or constant. While I acknowledge the validity and serious nature of legitimate mental illnesses, I disagree with the premise that every perpetual sickness or battle in the mind, consciousness, emotions, feelings, or thinking is the result of a mental illness.

What exactly would result in an official diagnosis of depression? According to the Diagnostic and Statistical Manual of Mental Disorders (DSM-5), a period of at least two weeks when someone experiences a depressed mood or loss of interest or pleasure in daily activities, in addition to a majority of specific symptoms, such as problems with sleep, eating, energy, concentration, or self-worth, would result in a diagnosis of depression.[32]

The lines between anxiety and depression are sometimes blurred. They are separately classified issues, but according to the American Journal of Psychiatry, their symptoms are frequently inseparable and they are suffered together almost 50% of the time. It's called *comorbidity*, which is the presence of two or more disorders in the same patient.[33] Additionally, there are four main overlapping symptoms: trouble sleeping, restlessness, fatigue, and trouble concentrating.[34] I was 4-for-4 a few times in my life. I don't believe that merits the label of mental illness.

Where Did It Begin?

There has been an abundance of research into this mindemic, resulting in a comprehensive understanding of the triggers and symptoms. For instance, anxiety will present with both physical and psychological symptoms. They include sweating, heart palpitations, nausea, shortness of breath, dry mouth, feeling fear or panic, obsessive thoughts, and flashbacks.[35]

Beyond the four overlapping symptoms we discussed, depression will present as feeling sad or anxious, feeling hopeless, irritability, changes in appetite or weight, unexplained pain, headaches, or digestive problems, and suicidal thoughts.[36]

These are not exhaustive lists but give you an idea of the wide range of ways anxiety and depression can affect you. The list of triggers that cause these symptoms is equally long. They include things like sudden life changes, loss, financial problems, relationship problems, etc. You could probably make your own list from life experience. This information is all fairly common and can be found in any medical journal or counseling website. None of this is surprising in the least.

My question, though, is where does it begin? What is the culprit that introduces this mindemic into a human being? What happens on the first day when an intrusive thought begins to plague the mind like a virus? What happens the first time someone feels hopeless and the feeling won't go away. How is it different from normal worry, stress, or sadness? Why do these things graduate to chronic intangible pain? Medical science has blamed chemical imbalances, side effects of medications, and genetics.[37] Psychology has blamed trauma, loss, and faulty childhood development. Neuroscience blames neurochemical abnormalities in the brain.[38] These are just a few of the theories available. Most experts agree, though, all this is just that: only theory. The hard fact is, the cause of anxiety and depression is *unknown*.

The Missing Link

Thus far in my investigation, I've yet to find definitive answers for three out of five of my questions. I'm not satisfied with theories and inconclusive research. Therefore, if the cause of the mindemic is unknown, the source of the pain is unknown, and it can't accurately be labeled, how can we possibly find a solution? I can't help but think we've overlooked something. The answer may be found in what we are *not* looking at.

Let's jump back for a moment to our discussion on the "hard problem." It's no secret that materialism (or physicalism) is the default belief of the sciences.[39] In light of that, it would lead one to deduce that scientific research into anxiety and depression is biased against dualism because they believe everything can be explained by brain function.

As a Christian, I personally lean toward the dualistic view. I believe, as evidence proves, that our conscious minds are not limited to our physical brains. But there's still something missing from the equation. Is it a mere coincidence that the origin of human consciousness and the cause of anxiety and depression are *both unknown* according to the sciences? I don't think so. In law enforcement, this is what's called a clue.

Herein lies my point. Dualism is partially correct, but it doesn't go far enough. We are not just body and mind. We are body, mind (soul), and *spirit*.[40] This opens a whole new realm of possibilities!

CHAPTER 3

Science vs. Faith

While researching and digesting the information, I discovered what appeared to be a standoff between science and faith. It became obvious that there is an inherent bias in medical science against faith. There are precious few in the field who dared to question the constructs of their modern medical training with talk of religion and spirituality.

Confirmation Bias

In criminal investigations, we call this *confirmation bias*. Confirmation bias occurs when an investigator believes or searches for evidence that supports his or her theory while dismissing exculpatory evidence. The investigator would then resist changing his or her belief once he or she arrives at a conclusion.[41]

If I were called to investigate a crime, I would examine every room of the crime scene for evidence. If another investigator pointed to a room and said, "Don't search that room." I would have to ask, "Why?" If the other investigator said, "We peeked into the room and didn't see anything," I would again have to respond with a question. "Is there evidence in that room that would solve the case?" The investigator inside me will not allow me to take the answers I'm given. My professional training and experience require me to keep gathering evidence, question and verify everything, and trust no one until the truth is uncovered.

Now imagine science is a crime scene divided into three rooms. Their job is to crack the case of anxiety and depression. One room represents the body or the study of medical science. The second room represents the mind or soul, and the third room represents the human spirit. Scientists are all over the "body" room searching for clues. They're beginning to dominate the "mind" room, but they are pointing to the "spirit" room and insisting, "Don't go in there. We don't know if the room contains evidence or not, but there's no need to look." Science is hesitant to look into the third room where the evidence may lie because it may not support the theories it has developed and then claims it can't find the exact cause of anxiety and depression.

It's like a homicide detective searching every room except one, then announcing he doesn't have any evidence to find the killer. If any detective in the country conducted his or her investigation in that manner, it would be unethical, immoral, and illegal. Yet, in its bias against religion and spirituality, the sciences seem to be doing just that.

The Divorce of Medicine and Faith

Only in the last century has there been a systematic cancellation of spirituality from the discipline of healthcare. In 1948, when the World Health Organization was formed, their founding documents defined health as "a state of complete physical, mental and social well-being, and not merely the absence of disease or infirmity." Decades later, during the 52nd Assembly of the W.H.O. in 1999, an amendment to the definition of health was presented and passed to include spiritual well-being. Unfortunately, it was vetoed.[42]

Why does this matter? What does spirituality have to do with health—physical, mental, or otherwise? History proves religion and spirituality are deeply rooted in the very origins of the practice of medicine. The first hospitals in the West were built by religious institutions. As far back as the middle ages, many physicians were also clergymen. The Monastery of St. Mary of Bethlehem built the world's first mental hospital in London in 1247. In fact, for centuries religious institutions were even responsible for licensing doctors to practice! In its earliest stages, medicine and religion were married.[43]

So, when and why did the divorce occur? You can thank Sigmund Freud for that. His mentor, Jean-Martin Charcot (1825-1893), considered to be the founder of modern neurology, was a professor of anatomy at the Salpêtrière Hospital in Paris. Charcot was hostile toward religion. He asserted that religious expressions were hysterical in nature. He also explained away all miracles and instances of faith healing to "hysterical suggestibility."[44] Freud, having been heavily influenced by Charcot, would go on to become a psychiatrist and neurologist and would shape mental health for the next century. Dr. Harold G. Koenig, Director of the Center for Spirituality, Theology, and Health at Duke University Medical Center writes, "He viewed religious beliefs and practices as a form of neurosis, something he would emphasize in writing that would span over three decades." In 1927, Freud wrote his most notable dissertation on religion, *Future of an Illusion*, in which he compared religious persons to those with mental retardation.[45] Even as early as the 1980s, Dr. Koenig wrote that religion and spirituality was seen as a neurotic crutch used only by the weak and mentally ill.[46]

Rediscovering the Forgotten Dimension

Despite this perceived inherent bias against religion and

spirituality, there are some in the field that have opened up the pandora's box of spirituality in their search for the truth. Recently, to their credit, medical academia has returned to studying the healing power of faith. According to doctors at Mayo Clinic, "Most studies have shown that religious involvement and spirituality are associated with better health outcomes, including greater longevity, coping skills, and health-related quality of life (even during terminal illness) and *less anxiety, depression, and suicide.*"[47]

There was a study conducted in the United Kingdom by John Swinton called, "Spirituality and Mental Healthcare: Rediscovering a Forgotten Dimension." In this study, people were interviewed about the relationship between their faith and their struggle with depression.

One participant said, "I don't depend on there being direct, individual meaning in my particular circumstances or situation. I'm quite happy to live with the idea that in a fallen world there are things that happen to people just sort of through chance and circumstance. But what one does need to believe is that all of that is happening in an ultimately meaningful framework. When I'm in a phase that I'm able to believe that there is a God who gives meaning to that universe, then I have hope."[48]

Another similar study, conducted at a psychiatric clinic in Langenthal, Switzerland, points to the reading of scripture as the method used by a 32-year-old man to cope with his depression. He said, "Reading Psalms helped me feel closer to God in difficult times." A 65-year-old woman in the same study cited prayer as the way she controlled her depression.[49]

Soul Sickness

I continued to uncover evidence that medical science is softening its indifference to spirituality. I read an article written by Dr. Charles R. Perakis, a family practitioner in Maine, that made me sit up in my seat. He reported treating patients who complained of vague, unexplained physical symptoms such as fatigue, sleeplessness, dizziness, and aches and pains. He suggested a diagnosis that is not found in any medical textbooks or journals. He called it, "soul sickness." He described it as a feeling of helplessness and hopelessness, perceived incompetence, and a general inability to cope with life stress. Dr. Perakis suggests that the cure for soul sickness is the resurgence of the patient's morale and hope.[50] You can imagine why this piqued my interest; it's the first piece of evidence I found in which a health professional pointed to something other than the brain as the source of the problem!

Dr. Perakis's unorthodox diagnosis did not come without scrutiny from the medical community. In a letter to the editor of the journal in which the article was published, a professor of psychiatry disagreed with the diagnosis, stating these types of patients have symptoms of a "serious mood disorder."[51] This further solidified my impression that healthcare professionals, by and large, still insist on approaching everything from a physicalist viewpoint, denying any notion that something else might be at play.

Nevertheless, I was excited to see this dialog taking place. It was encouraging to see someone in the medical field at least acknowledging that intangible pain doesn't necessarily mean something was wrong with the brain. This missing piece of evidence is the string that began to pull all of my questions together.

Expert Witness

I wanted to talk to this doctor who was brass enough to color outside the proverbial lines. I was interested to know how he arrived at this diagnosis of soul sickness, and I considered him to be an expert witness. Now retired, Dr. Perakis lives in a suburb outside Portland, Maine. When I reached out to him, he was generous enough to grant me an interview.

I began my interview by referring to Dr. Perakis's article in the Journal of the American Osteopathic Association. Specifically, I was interested in how he arrived at this soul sickness diagnosis. From the very beginning, he addressed one of my problems with mental health: labels. He compared the traditional labels of mental illness to the stickers placed on items at the local department store. When you try to peel off the label, you can never get it all off. It always sticks.

"How did I get to where I am?" He continued, "It evolved. I went into family medicine, even after being discouraged to do so in a number of ways. My mentor whispered in my ear as I was receiving my degree, 'Specialize.' I would talk to students who would say, 'Don't go into family medicine; that's for losers.' So immediately you see the mindset of the medical field. I didn't specialize. I am very much a believer in holistic medicine."

I asked, "You're a D.O., aren't you?" He replied in the affirmative. It's important to note that a D.O., or Doctor of Osteopathic Medicine, is a fully-licensed physician who uses a "whole person" approach to medicine. They are trained to listen and partner with patients to help them get healthy and stay well.[52]

Dr. Perakis continued to paint the picture of his medical philosophy so I could better understand how he arrived at this idea of soul sickness. "It evolved as I took care of people who were poor, in an underserved area, who didn't have much in the way resources. I came to find that a lot of this stuff we have (stress, anxiety, depression) comes from predicaments. You might call the pandemic the ultimate predicament. Everybody is touched by it, and I view it as an opportunity because it has exposed a lot of what's wrong. We've all had soul sickness before."

What he said made a lot of sense to me, and closely resembled my own persuasion that a lot of the intangible pain we deal with is a result of undesirable events that occur in our lives and, therefore, don't necessarily deserve the label of mental illness.

I was interested to hear his perspective on the subject at hand. "What is your view on the relationship between anxiety, depression, and what I'm calling 'intangible pain' and 'human consciousness'?"

Dr. Perakis corrected me. "I would try to avoid the term, 'depression.' When I was in practice and had to label things, I would call it 'anxiety/depression,' because sometimes I couldn't tell which was which. And, there are often elements of some in everyone. There is an element of depression that responds very well to antidepressants. That's why these antidepressants are so popular. That's an inherited form of depression, in my opinion—a genetic type of depression. If you look at family history, you will see it, and it can be very serious. These medications can change that completely. Antidepressants are way over-used for reactive depression."

This is the first time in my investigation I had heard the term, *reactive depression*, also called *situational depression*. It is simply depression precipitated by events in a person's life.[53] While reading all this research, I had cognitively distinguished between major depression as a mental illness versus depression caused by *predicaments*, as Dr. Perakis called it, but now I had a name for it. This put things into perspective for me.

His comment on antidepressants prompted me to take a fork in the road and ask him about a related statistic I had recently read. "Dr. Perakis, I read that 73% of healthcare visits in which an antidepressant was prescribed to medical patients, no anxiety or depression diagnosis was reported. This is evidence that antidepressants are over-prescribed."[54]

He quickly shot back, "They are also used to treat insomnia, which is a symptom of depression. That's what we do with a lot of things, is treat symptoms. It's a very lucrative endeavor for physicians; that's part of the problem. Look what happened with the misuse of opioids; that's a classic example. It's terrible."

Speaking with Dr. Perakis gave me the impression he was independent in his thinking and didn't jump on every medical bandwagon that rolled into town. He confirmed that when he said to me he had always been an upstream swimmer in his field, and never went with the tide. He began to explain his approach to holism in his practice of medicine.

"In medicine, the doctor interrupts the patient within 14 seconds of them starting the conversation; it's been studied. When a person comes to me with a headache or ADHD or whatever their complaint, I have a whole process of history taking. I call it history *making* so I can involve the patient's story. I listen to the patient. They tell me their story. I interpret their story, and they do what they want with it."

Then he asked me a question. "What is the number one rule of medicine? Do you have any idea?" I said, "Me? No." He continued with the lesson, "I'm not surprised, but it's important. *Primum non nocere*. It means, 'first, do no harm.' In other words, don't make matters worse. Be cautious about what you do because there are consequences. A lot of the medicine in this country is iatrogenic, which means, induced by the physician. What happened with narcotics is a perfect example of that—the ultimate, terrible, perfect example." "So, holism," he concluded, "is the relationship between the parts."

I pressed Dr. Perakis on his view of human consciousness. After all, there was part of me that believed intangible pain was a resident of the mind or soul and didn't necessarily relate to a brain problem.

"I've looked at this a lot," he said. "Who's the thinker of the thought? I have that voice in my head; some people would say it's the ego. It has elements of good and evil; it's a human primal thing. We can't waste our time worrying about what consciousness is because I don't think there's an answer to that."

Dr. Perakis explained that he is in a place in his life when he is focused on the present. He said, "I like to use the term, 'negative capability.' You probably haven't heard that term, but it exemplifies where my answers come from. John Keats, the poet, wrote a letter to his brother using the term 'negative capability'—the ability to live in mystery and doubt without the obsessive search for fact and reason. Do you see? That's the mystery I can live with. I have 'negative capability.'"

He continued, putting the point on the exclamation. "I want to be in the present. Ram Dass wrote years ago, 'Be Here Now.' It's trite, but it's the answer. If you live in the present, you don't have to worry about the past or the future. Most anxiety and depression comes from worrying about the past and the future."

As I pondered what Dr. Perakis was saying, it seemed to drip with philosophical thought. When he told me he obtained a Master's Degree in Education after medical school, it made sense. He went on to discuss expressive arts therapy as a treatment for soul sickness. He said, "Expressive arts therapy is a road to the soul." After chatting a bit more, Dr. Perakis concluded our discussion with this, "A good question is worth a handful of answers."

As I processed the interview, I revisited a couple of specific statements the doctor made. The first was this idea of *negative capability*. He was right, I had never heard that term before. I repeated the definition back to myself, "The ability to live in mystery and doubt without the obsessive search for fact and reason." I thought, "If you remove the word, 'doubt,'" that sounds a lot like faith." As a believer, that's what I have to do every day: to be content to live in uncertainty without being obsessed about the how and why.

The other thing that captured my attention specifically was his comment on expressive arts therapy, which he called, "the road to the soul." My mind immediately went to scripture in 1 Samuel 16:23:

> *"Whenever the tormenting spirit from God troubled Saul, David would play the harp. Then Saul would feel better, and the tormenting spirit would go away."*

Dr. Perakis wrote the article on soul sickness twelve years ago, but he was still very much enthusiastic about its implications. Although our religious beliefs differ, we connected on these two pillars. He calls them negative capability and expressive arts therapy. I call them faith and worship. Either way, they are indeed the road to the soul.

I had one more expert witness to interview, but I was beginning to see a pattern developing.

CHAPTER 4

The Limits of Medical Science

I previously quoted a man who is largely responsible for the remarriage of science and faith. Going out on a limb, I reached out by email to request an interview. To my surprise, I received a response within the hour.

Expert Witness

I had the privilege of meeting and interviewing the world's foremost expert on the subject of religion and spirituality in mental health. Dr. Harold G. Koenig is Professor of Psychiatry, Associate Professor of Medicine, and Director of the Center for Spirituality, Theology, and Health at Duke University Medical Center in Durham, North Carolina. He's an Adjunct Professor in the Department of Medicine at King Abdulaziz University in Jeddah, Saudi Arabia, and Adjunct Professor of Public Health at Ningxia Medical University in Yinchuan, P.R. China. He is also a Visiting Professor at Shiraz University of Medical Sciences in Shiraz, Iran.

Dr. Koenig has authored more than 50 books, including *Religion and Mental Health: Research and Clinical Applications*, *The Handbook on Religion and Health*, *Christianity and*

Psychiatry, and *The Healing Power of Prayer*. He has contributed chapters to more than 90 books, authored 19 professional manuals, and written more than 500 articles published in the *Journal of American Geriatrics Society, Journal of Family Practice, Journal of Internal Medicine, International Journal of Psychiatry in Medicine, Journal of Geriatric Psychiatry, American Journal of Psychiatry, Journal of the American Medical Association, American Journal of Family Therapy, Christian Counseling Today*, and a host of others too numerous to list here.

Dr. Koenig has made more than 60 national television appearances including *Dr. Oz, ABC World News Tonight, NBC Nightly News*, and multiple appearances on *The Today Show* and *Good Morning America*. He was invited to testify before the U.S. Senate Appropriations Subcommittee in 1998 on the health effects of religious belief and prayer and before the United Nations in New York in 1999 on religious impact on health. He also consulted with the U.S. Army to develop a training curriculum for chaplains in Special Operations Command (SOCOM).

Dr. Koenig has been the recipient of at least 45 prestigious professional awards including *Best Doctors in America, America's Top Psychiatrists*, and multiple nominations for the *Templeton Prize in Religion*.

This is only a highlight reel, as Dr. Koenig's resume is about 105 pages long and growing. It's safe to say he is *the* expert on the subject of religion, spirituality, and mental health. Period. On top of all of that, he's very humble, energetic, and kind; a true Christian gentleman.

I wanted to make the best use of my limited time with Dr. Koenig; as you can probably imagine, he's a very busy man. After our introductory pleasantries, I fired off the first question that had been bothering me during this process.

"Dr. Koenig, is it your opinion that medical science, specifically in the realm of psychiatry, tends to be inherently biased against religion and spirituality? And do you see that changing?"

My expert witness didn't waste any time and didn't even have to ponder the question. "Well, I think there's a long historical tradition of bias against religion, starting with Sigmund Freud, who wrote about religion as a universal obsessive neurosis. That has flavored the practice of mental health professionals for the last 100 years. Also, how did people cope with depression and anxiety for thousands of years of human existence before mental health care professionals came around? It was through religion, religious beliefs, and practice. That's how they dealt with stress and change and loss."

I guess I expected Dr. Koenig to approach his answer with a hint of respectful defense, given I had just fired a shot across his bow. On the contrary, he completely verified my assumption! Then he blindsided me with a point I had not considered.

"So really, the professional mental health field is the new guy on the block in many respects. These are kind of parallel systems where, probably, most people are coping through religious activities and beliefs. They're going to their pastor to discuss their issues, while a small proportion of people are going to see psychiatrists, mental health professionals, and counselors."

"Do you mean to tell me," I thought, "that clergy have more impact on mental health in America than mental health professionals?" He had just validated the ministry as a first-string starter in this ball game. It was affirming, to say the least. He went on to answer the second half of my question.

"There is a big divide between the two (religion and spirituality

36

vs. mental health care), but it is becoming closer, based on the enormous amount of scientific, objective, qualifiable research that has been documented."

Now, I consider myself to be a pretty intimidating interrogator/interviewer, but this guy didn't hesitate in the least. He had dominated this discussion right off the bat. I decided to hit him with another question I was trying to get to the bottom of.

"I've read a lot about the mind-body problem, or what has been called the 'hard problem.' What is your view on the relationship between anxiety and depression and human consciousness? Where does depression live?" Once again, I was not prepared for his answer.

"Well, the only thing that we can study, that science can study, is that which is objective and verifiable. If it's not objective and verifiable, then science has no way to address it. Anxiety and depression do live in the brain." He repeated that point. "They live in the brain. There are biochemical changes that occur within the brain, partly as a result of inherited temperaments, that put people at risk for experiencing anxiety and depression. There are medications and psychotherapies that can help to actually change the brain chemicals to a point that a person is less distressed and the less upset about it."

"Medicine or psychological therapies that focus on how people think and behave are both helpful because the way you think and behave largely influences those biochemical changes in the brain. Religion is very cognitive behavior. It's about belief and behaviors: what you should and shouldn't do. I think cognitive behavioral therapy is actually really based upon the Scriptures."

In preparation for my interview with Dr. Koenig, I wanted to get to know more about him personally, so I picked up one of his books entitled, *You Are My Beloved. Really?* I read it the night before our interview.

I said, "Dr. Koenig I can tell by reading your book that you are a man of strong faith."

He interrupted me. This accomplished physician, scientist, and researcher allowed his humanity to peek through for a moment. "I struggle with my faith. I mean, even Mother Theresa struggled with her faith and wrote about it. Anybody with a scientific brain who's digging into this stuff is going to be challenged with their faith. Every day I struggle."

He went on to explain how his faith compels him to correctly represent his research. "Bias is a real problem, particularly for scientists. All scientists are biased in some way, but I have to be very careful so that I do not allow my bias to influence what I'm doing in my work. I feel that's part of my religious belief—that I can't be lying or exaggerating [my research]. That wouldn't be right. So, I try as best I can to provide both sides."

I changed gears a little and explained to Dr. Koenig where I was in my investigation. I asked him to talk to me about his scientific research and how it points toward religion and spirituality as a treatment for depression and anxiety.

"We have done randomized controlled trials and developed several religious interventions for the treatment of depression, anxiety, and moral injury. Some would call it the injury of the soul, but we call it moral injury. Moral injury is a component of the PTSD that veterans suffer as a result of their combat experience. So, we've developed Bible-based interventions to treat depression, anxiety, and moral injury."

So far, this interview had filled in some blanks for me. Dr. Koenig was easy to interview; his answers came swiftly and precisely. But I was still waiting for a smoking gun from the expert witness to validate my developing theory. I never even got to ask the question. He fired first.

"There is no question that a religious-oriented, cognitive-behavioral type of treatment for depression and anxiety, particularly in religious individuals, is helpful. It has a large effect in reducing symptoms."

It was almost as if I could hear the boom of the cannon! It's always a good feeling when a witness gives you something to crack the case wide open. Have you ever watched cops high-five on television? We actually do that in moments of epiphany like this.

After the sparks fizzled out, though, I realized I wasn't out of the woods yet. He had said something earlier in the interview that I was still stuck on. *Depression lives in the brain.* He said it twice to drive home the point. I'll be honest, that's not what I wanted or expected to hear. Almost everything I had read so far had led me in the direction of the mind-body dilemma, causing me to deduce that anxiety and depression, though they affect the brain, are problems of the mind, the soul, human consciousness (remember I have used these interchangeably).

I decided to press Dr. Koenig a little further on this question. "Connect for me this idea of human consciousness, or the mind, with anxiety and depression. You said that depression lives in the brain. Do you believe there's also an element of depression that lives in human consciousness that can't necessarily be treated by medicine?"

"That's a good point certainly, but how do you differentiate that? There is definitely treatment-resistant depression where, no matter what you give a patient, they don't respond. A lot of times that is driven by genetics—the genes that are inherited—and early life experiences that seem to interact with those genes produce depression. And even developmentally, it produces brain changes that result in treatment-resistant depression. So again, these terms, 'soul,' 'mind,' 'consciousness,' how do you differentiate those? There's no way you can prove that because it's outside of science; outside of time and space. How do you reframe or try to constrict God to a box and then try to measure what God is doing? You can't; it's impossible. All you can study are the benefits that religious faith has and show that by using religious intervention to heal someone, and do it in a systematic way."

The Cliff of Medical Science

He wouldn't budge, yet he had helped me understand something important. Science can only address what is objective and verifiable. When I pondered that, I realized what he was saying. The limitations of science are the limitations of science. It cannot study human consciousness because there are no quantifiable variables to study. It cannot study the human spirit because there are no quantifiable variables to study. He was telling me what he could verify: that anxiety and depression do live in the brain, and we know that because we can verify that with objective, quantifiable research. That is not to say depression and anxiety don't affect the mind (soul) or spirit, just that there is no way to test something that is outside the limitations of science.

His question reverberated in my mind, "How do you reframe or try to constrict God to a box, and then try to measure what God is doing?" It reminded me of these words found in Ecclesiastes 3:11:

> *"He has planted eternity in the human heart, but even so, people cannot see the whole scope of God's work from beginning to end."*

Something suddenly clicked for me. I was interviewing the

person who was pushing the limits of science as far as they would go in the area of mental health; the person who received resistance from his colleagues when he began to research religion, spirituality, and mental health in the 1980s but went on to distinguish himself as the expert in the field. He was on the edge of this discipline. No, he was *leaning over* the edge. I wanted to see that edge. Dr. Koenig had just given me homework. By the time I realized it, it was too late.

"Where can I find your research on religious intervention?" Dr. Koenig held up a large, thick book and said, "This guy right here," referring me to his own *Religion and Mental Health: Research and Clinical Applications.* Remembering that he's an academic, I said, "That looks like a textbook, doc." He said, "It's not too bad."

After our interview, I went straight to his book and started digging. It contains a treasure trove of research about how religious beliefs and practices change the brain and improve anxiety and depression. It was about what can be measured. Dr. Koenig divides religious intervention into two basic types. "(1) interventions that use religious beliefs/practices alone to affect mental health and (2) religious psychotherapies."[55] As I sifted through the information, I suddenly had a familiar feeling of studying for a test in college. Turns out, it's a textbook, as I had suspected.

CHAPTER 5

The Case for Science

I dove into Dr. Koenig's homework assignment with enthusiasm. He had awakened me to the reunion of mental health science and faith. His study, and that of others, began to fill in the blanks of my own personal understanding. I was beginning to wrap my brain around this mindemic and was both surprised and challenged by what I found. In this chapter, the case will be presented for the integration of religion and spirituality with mental health care and its impact on anxiety, depression, and other intangible pain.

The evidence presented is objective. It has no preference, no bias, no emotion, no opinion. Evidence is evidence; nothing more, nothing less. However, in some instances, evidence has to be interpreted. Interpretation is subjective based on the preference, bias, emotion, and opinion of the interpreter. This is what can lead to confirmation bias (as I discussed in the last chapter).

Remember when I said earlier that my own belief system would be challenged by what I found? This is where I begin to take you through that process. No attempt will be made to skew the evidence to fit personal beliefs; that would negate the purpose of this book. I encourage you to approach this information with an open mind, as I have, and make your own determination.

What Do We Mean?

Some of the research cited uses universal terms such as "religion," "spirituality," "prayer," and "intervention"; these words are also often combined. Some of these words may be associated with negative connotations. It's important to clarify them as used in this chapter.

Religion. Especially in evangelical circles, the words *religion* or *religious* often have negative connotations, having been used to describe the robotic nature of ritualism or liturgy, which believers feel doesn't rise to the level of a relationship with God. In other words, religion and relationship are viewed as different, and relationship is what believers are seeking. *Religion* is sometimes seen as "Pharisaical," as relating to the Pharisees of the New Testament who glorified their ritual laws above the teachings of Jesus. If when you hear the word "religion" it invokes negative emotions, I encourage you to set those aside and hear the word differently in this chapter.

Here is the definition I want you to consider: *Religion is the belief in and worship (practices, rituals) of a personal God.*[56]

Spirituality. The word spirituality is used to describe many things across many different faith disciplines. For our purposes, we will use the following definition of spirituality based upon Christian faith. *Spirituality, that which is at the core of religion, is God, outside of the self, and yet also within the self. Spirituality is the cause of belief in and worship of God.*[57]

Prayer. "Prayer is not [meditation], mental telepathy or autosuggestion. It is not magic, psychic energy, or human intentionality. Prayer is not merely thinking good thoughts. It is not repeating nonsense syllables, doing breathing exer- cises, or practicing visualization."[58] [59] *Prayer is a* *conversation with God.*

Intervention. There are many variations of interventions. Perhaps you have experience with a friend or family member whose life is being affected by substance abuse, and your family staged an intervention. This is called a *crisis intervention.*[60] A simple definition of intervention, in terms of mental health, is *any action intended to change the medical or behavioral outcome for a patient.*[61] In this chapter, we will specifically discuss religious interventions.

Before going any further, it is critical that you consider this caveat. There is an abundance of published research on this subject—some compelling, some not so much (consider the source). The important thing is that you see it for what it is: science. Science cannot account for the miracle factor. There is no test for the supernatural,[62] yet the evidence of God's supernatural intervention or divine healing is overwhelming. We'll talk more about that in the next chapter, *The Case for Faith*.

Religious Interventions

Keep in mind, this chapter is not intended to exhaust the subject of religious interventions but to highlight the research in a way that will encourage you to take personal action. As a gentle reminder, this is not a science book or a mental health textbook. I am not a mental health professional. I am an investigator making a case for healing. This is where it gets real.

As stated in the last chapter, Dr. Koenig divides religious intervention into two basic types: (1) those that use religious beliefs and practices alone to improve mental health and (2) religious psychotherapies.[63] Don't be intimidated by the word *psychotherapies*; it simply refers to specific methods of counseling used by mental health professionals.

There are five types of psychotherapies used in religious intervention. We'll take a closer look at two of them: *pastoral care* and *religious counseling*. Pastoral care is just what it sounds like. It is conducted by local pastors whose congregants come to them for spiritual advice. It can also be conducted by chaplains who have clinical pastoral education (CPE). Religious counseling is very similar but is conducted by licensed professional counselors.[64]

In both cases, methods are used to help those suffering from anxiety and depression that have proven to be very effective. Those methods include prayer, reading of scripture, teaching scriptural principles, and, specifically, praying and believing for divine healing.[65] As I write this, it seems so elementary and basic to me that prayer and the Word of God are effective in overcoming intangible pain. I have to keep reminding myself that this information is being examined in a clinical framework. Science has proven that religious beliefs and practices—so basic to believers—are effective!

Prayer

It has been argued that we are genetically predisposed to the need for prayer; therefore, the reason we pray is that we cannot help but pray.[66] It is the dialogue between the Creator and His creation.

Prayer is a primary religious practice with unmistakably profound power. Believers certainly do not need scientific evidence of this power, because we have personal life experiences that serve as irrefutable evidence. It is certainly no surprise that scientific evidence supports that belief.

A study was conducted using randomized, controlled trials involving 63 primary care medical patients with anxiety and depression symptoms. For six weeks, a Christian lay minister prayed for each person in the randomized group in-person once a week for six weeks. The first session was 90 minutes and included a discussion between the lay minister and the patient about the specific areas for which prayer was needed. The remaining sessions were 60 minutes each. The results of the trial were unmistakable, showing a significant reduction in anxiety and depression symptoms. This improvement was maintained twelve months after the study. The patients in the control group were on a waiting list to undergo the prayer session. Prior to being "crossed over" into the prayer group, the control group patients received "treatment as usual." They showed no change in symptoms.[67]

Another study was conducted to determine the effects of remote intercessory prayer on cardiac patients at San Francisco General Hospital. A randomized, controlled study of 393 patients in which 192 patients were assigned to a Christian intercessory prayer group not affiliated with the hospital found that they did significantly better than the 201 people in the control group. The results were called "miraculous."[68]

Scripture

Christians believe the Bible is the divinely inspired Word of God. Within its pages are the information and inspiration needed to live a fulfilled, Christ-like life. The Scriptures contain a great deal of teachings about beliefs and behaviors. It's only reasonable to expect them to be effective in pastoral care and religious counseling, in the framework of psychotherapy, to improve symptoms of anxiety and depression. The writings of the Apostle Paul to Timothy point to the purpose of Scripture in correcting these wrong beliefs and behaviors.

"All Scripture is inspired by God and is useful to teach us what is true and to make us realize what is wrong in our lives. It corrects us when we are wrong

and teaches us to do what is right." (2 Timothy 3:16)

According to Dr. Koenig, when administering religiously-integrated cognitive behavioral therapy for depression in Christians, scriptures can be used to challenge dysfunctional thoughts and underlying beliefs that are enabling the depression, replacing them with healthy Bible-based beliefs and behaviors.[69] Paul's writings to the Romans encourage them to allow God to change the way they think:

> *"Don't copy the behavior and customs of this world, but let God transform you into a new person by changing the way you think. Then you will learn to know God's will for you, which is good and pleasing and perfect." (Romans 12:2)*

When he wrote to the Philippians, Paul echoed this principle to them as well:

> *"And now, dear brothers and sisters, one final thing. Fix your thoughts on what is true, and honorable, and right, and pure, and lovely, and admirable. Think about things that are excellent and worthy of praise." (Philippians 4:8)*

The same theme continued to ring through in his letter to the Ephesians:

> *"Let the Spirit renew your thoughts and attitudes." (Ephesians 4:23)*

The message continues in his letter to the Colossians:

> *"Think about the things of heaven, not the things of earth." (Colossians 3:2)*

And his letter to the Corinthians:

> *"We use God's mighty weapons, not worldly weapons,*

to knock down the strongholds of human reasoning and to destroy false arguments. We destroy every proud obstacle that keeps people from knowing God. We capture their rebellious thoughts and teach them to obey Christ." (2 Corinthians 10:4-5)

The Apostle Paul's teachings touched on God's desire to replace anxiety with His peace in our minds:

"Don't worry about anything; instead, pray about everything. Tell God what you need, and thank him for all he has done. Then you will experience God's peace, which exceeds anything we can understand. His peace will guard your hearts and minds as you live in Christ Jesus." (Romans 4:6-7)

This is a consistent and powerful theme in Paul's epistles. It is a strong message to every believer: Be careful as to what you allow into your mind! Why is Paul so concerned about this? He answers that question in his letter to the Romans:

"So, letting your sinful nature control your mind leads to death. But letting the Spirit control your mind leads to life and peace." (Romans 8:6)

The scriptures have the power to change our thoughts and behaviors. Why does religious intervention work? Neuroplasticity. Neuroscientist Dr. Andrew Newberg defines it as "the ability of the human brain to structurally rearrange itself in response to a wide variety of positive and negative events."[70] This is how prayer and scripture transform the brain.

Religious Doubt

Have you ever questioned your belief in God? Have you ever struggled with your faith? Have you ever wrestled with religious questions for which you have no answers? Have you ever had the experience of being mad at God because of negative events that occurred in your life? Have you ever wondered why God answers some prayers but doesn't answer others? If so, did it make you feel guilty, ashamed, or unfaithful to struggle with those religious doubts? You're not alone.

Scientific evidence connects religious doubt with poor mental health. A review of 52 case studies revealed 87% of them reported negative religious coping (religious doubt) causes poor mental health.[71] The question left unanswered by research is: Does religious doubt cause anxiety, depression, and emotional distress, or do depression, anxiety, and emotional distress cause religious doubt?[72] It's the age-old chicken or egg question.

A specific study published in the International Journal for the Psychology of Religion concluded that anxiety most likely leads to an increase in religious doubt, rather than religious doubt causing an increase in anxiety.[73] I find this very interesting given what happened in the Garden of Eden in Genesis (see the final chapter). However, that study has been countered by others that show little to no correlation. Therefore, just like the chicken and the egg, this question is still unresolved.

Genetic Predispositions

So far we've established that religious intervention reduces the effects of anxiety and depression; specifically, pastoral care and religious counseling using prayer and scripture reading. This is great news for those who suffer from situational depression caused by external and environmental factors. But what about those who suffer from depression brought about by genetic predispositions?

Just such a study was conducted by scientists at Columbia University in New York City. They studied 114 subjects over a 10-year period, consisting of those with depressed parents and non-depressed parents. Those who stated that religion and spirituality were "very important" to them were 73% less likely to become depressed, in contrast to subjects who stated religion and spirituality were "somewhat" or "not important." Additionally, high-risk subjects, due to parental depression, who stated religion and spirituality were "very important" were 90% less likely to develop depression.[74]

Being a genetically high-risk individual doesn't always mean you will suffer from anxiety and depression. It simply means that if your parents and/or grandparents suffered, you may have received their genes that predispose you, also. However, Dr. Koenig points out that those genetic predispositions in mental health are seldom deterministic (like eye color, facial features, etc.). You don't have to align with genetic predispositions to anxiety and depression. I believe you can break the generational curse!

De Facto Shrinks

There's something I haven't yet disclosed to you. In addition to spending two decades in the field of law enforcement, I am a "de facto shrink." I will reiterate to you, I'm not a licensed clinical counselor, psychologist, or physician, but I am an ordained minister. Pastoral care and religious counseling have been in my wheelhouse since 1996. Having the benefit of these two careers converging in my life gives me a unique perspective on mental health—a view from the front line if you will.

In my interview with Dr. Koenig, he asked me, "How did people cope with depression and anxiety before mental health care professionals came around?" In his book, *Faith and Mental Health*, he writes, "Prior to the rise of professional mental health care systems, it was religious organizations that provided a "de facto" mental health system for populations around the world.[75] In fact, clergy in the United States are on the front line in terms of providing mental health services, delivering almost as much counseling as the entire membership of the American Psychological Association.[76] [77]

Conducting this investigation enlightened me even more about the impact of my own work in mental health through the years. Teaching the scriptures, visiting homes and hospitals to provide in-person prayer for anyone who would allow me, discipling believers, counseling individuals and families in crisis, encouraging the discouraged, and the list goes on. While I don't always see it as mental health care, that's exactly what it is. Ministry has always been in the business of speaking hope and peace to the minds of people.

I learned something, though, about the importance of follow-up as it relates to congregants who have stopped coming to church. It may not be that the pastor said something they didn't agree with or that they've had a conflict with someone in the church. It may be that they are battling depression, and their depression has reduced their desire or willingness to engage in religious practices.[78] If your pastor is trying to reach you, he or she may be concerned about your mental health.

The Remarriage of Science and Faith

As we've already discussed, the grandfathers of mental health discouraged religious involvement, dismissing it as the *product* of mental illness rather than a treatment strategy. However, while mental health experts believe religion is only for the mentally ill, a contingency of the church considers mental health care only for those who are weak. I guess the road goes both ways. As a representative of clergy, I always held to the general belief that mental health was taboo, a result of sin in the world, and even demonic in some cases. Without judgment or condemnation of those who sought mental health care, I privately believed that taking medication was a sign of that weakness, and healing should be sought from God. My personal experience with chronic stress, anxiety, and depression, however, drove me into this investigation to find more answers. It sharply challenged and ultimately reformed my belief system.

Armed with this new knowledge I began to believe that religion and spirituality have to work in tandem with medical science, rather than being at odds with it.

For the past century, objective, verifiable research has been published to make a strong case for the remarriage of religion and spirituality and mental health care. The findings are undeniable regardless of one's belief system. As Dr. Perakis wrote, the cure for what he calls "soul sickness" is a restoration of hope. "Without hope," Dr. Koenig writes, "few people will strive to make the painful changes necessary to maintain or enhance their health."[79] Hope is exactly what faith in God provides.

Devotion to God, studies have found, decreases the connection between stressful life events and extreme anxiety.[80] There is also evidence that religious intervention (prayer, scripture reading, teaching of scripture) is more effective in clients who are religious than those who are not.[81] After reviewing this evidence, it is easy to deduce that the case for science makes an even stronger case for faith! That's what we will do next.

CHAPTER 6

The Case for Faith

T he truth of Dr. Koenig's assertions during our interview left me with a question. Where do we go when we have exhausted all evidence and come to the *cliff* of medical science? The answer is found in faith. Again, there is no test or trial for the supernatural, but if there is a strong case for science, there is a stronger case for faith.

The Paradox of Faith

"Faith" is another word that has a broad definition and means different things to people of different beliefs. I use "faith" in the Christian sense of the word: a belief in God and trust in his ability to act on my behalf. The Bible specifically defines faith; that definition is found in Hebrews 11:1:

> *"Now faith is the substance of things hoped for, the evidence of things not seen." (NKJV)*

Science gives us evidence we can see, but faith gives us evidence we can't see. This is a paradox. It doesn't make sense. The very definition of evidence seems to conflict with this use of the word in Scripture. Evidence, when found, is a conspicuous outward sign, or proof, of the truth. By its very nature, evidence always looks back in time. On the other hand, faith, by its very nature, looks ahead in time. It is impossible to have evidence of something that *hasn't* happened, and unnecessary to have faith in something that has *already* happened. Yet, this is the paradox of faith.

Perhaps this is why many people struggle with having faith. It's difficult to comprehend faith as something more than an abstract idea, or belief in something that *may* happen, but faith is more than that. Faith is evidence in eternity of something that is yet to happen in time.

How can something intangible like faith be evidence? Think of it in terms of a witness providing testimony in a trial. That witness's testimony is only as good as their credibility. The witness has to be believed in order for their testimony to become evidence in the case. In other words, the court has to trust the witness. The witness, in this case, is God Himself. Consider this verse from Hebrews as a statement of God's credibility.

> *"When God made his promise to Abraham, since there was no one greater for him to swear by, he swore by himself, saying, 'I will surely bless you and give you many descendants.' And so after waiting patiently, Abraham received what was promised."*
> *(Hebrews 6:13-15)*

The Jewish nation is one of the proofs that God's promise to Abraham did, in fact, come to pass. It is an undisputed fact. This means there is historical evidence of God's credibility. God has a track record of doing what He says He will do. Therefore, as a witness, He is more credible than any witness. He is so credible that He swore by himself because there was no one greater or higher in authority to swear by. Is it any wonder that witnesses in a court of law have to swear on a Bible that they will tell the truth and that those sworn into office must take their oath with their hands upon the Bible?

Faith, therefore, is evidence of what God has done that we cannot see or looking forward to what God has promised to do that is yet to happen.

What is beyond the realm and capability of science to prove is proven by the evidence of our Creator's testimony, which has proven to be credible. Where scientific evidence reaches its limit, faith evidence takes over.

I respect medical science. I respect those who have dedicated their lives to helping people who are diseased, in pain, and otherwise suffering. However, I think we have become so accustomed to leaning on medical science that we forget there is another dimension that connects us with our Creator.

Despite the extensive research on the books, the root cause of anxiety and depression is yet unknown. Even scientists who once held a physicalist view, which dismisses the existence of the mind or human spirit, have been led by their very own research in the direction of the Creator. That takes faith!

We've examined the evidence, such as that presented by Dr. Dean Hamer in his book, *The God Gene*, that human beings have a genetic predisposition to seek the divine. We've also examined evidence that faith and spirituality contribute to health—both physically and mentally. To ignore any or all of this evidence would jeopardize our ability to crack the case for healing.

Modern medical science is continually advancing but will never exist outside its own realm. In terms of mental health, medical science can treat the brain but not the mind (soul) or spirit because they exist in a different realm. And just as the body, mind (soul), and spirit work together, medicine and religion and spirituality must also work together. Healing from anxiety depression and other intangible pain requires a multidimensional approach.

It's clear that scientists can be biased, philosophers can be biased, and even theologians can be biased—each with their own persuasion. But someone who wants to know the hard truth, even if it disagrees with their presumptions, belief systems, and established theories, will look at all of the evidence and rule out nothing.

When I began this journey for answers I already had a theory, but I have allowed my theory to be tested by the evidence, rather than the other way around. No rational person, having looked at the evidence for himself can intelligently conclude that religion and spirituality (i.e., God) is not involved in the healing process. If you are beginning to be persuaded, you're practicing faith!

Case Studies

If you look closely, you will discover that the Bible has much to say about mental health. Interwoven into the physical healing miracles of scripture are vivid accounts of how God provided mental and emotional healing.

The New Testament is full of those healing stories. For three and a half years, Jesus of Nazareth spread healing wherever He went—from the synagogues to the streets to the homes of His followers. He healed blindness, deafness, palsy, paralysis, leprosy, fever, and many other afflictions. He even raised people from the dead! He became so popular for these incidents of unexplained, supernatural healing that he was sought out by all those who were sick and oppressed. Crowds gathered everywhere he went.

Jesus' healing miracles are evidence beyond that which can be explained by medical science. You will clearly see the theme of mental health shine through in each story. They are evidence in the case for faith.

Case 1: The Invalid

In the 5th chapter of John's Gospel, we are introduced to an invalid man who was lying near the pool of Bethesda outside Jerusalem. We do not know his age, but we are told he has been in this condition for 38 years. The exact nature of his condition is unknown. The only indication we are given is in the original Greek text of the scripture, which uses two words to describe his problem. In verse 5, the word used is asthéneia, and in verse 7, the word used is asthenéō. Both are translated "without strength" likely due to illness.[82] Verse 6 says that the man is lying down, which suggests he cannot stand up because of the weakness in his legs.

For these 38 years, he has been laying at the Pool of Bethesda, a place just outside the city of Jerusalem that was built under ancient Roman rule. Though the name means, "House of Mercy," ironically it was not a temple or a synagogue. It was an Asclepion, a healing center dedicated to Asclepius, the Greco-Roman god of healing.[83] Historians, archeologists and theologians believe it to be a place where the sick and diseased gathered to seek the "mercy" of the mythical god. The associated healing rituals would often involve non-venomous snakes that would roam freely in the Asclepion.[84] The symbol of the Rod of Asclepius, a snake entwined stick, survived for centuries and became the universal symbol of modern healthcare.[85]

> *"Afterward Jesus returned to Jerusalem for one of the Jewish holy days. Inside the city, near the Sheep Gate, was the pool of Bethesda, with five covered porches. Crowds of sick people—blind, lame, or paralyzed— lay on the porches. One of the men lying there had been sick for thirty-eight years. When Jesus saw him and knew he had been ill for a long time, he asked him, 'Would you like to get well?' 'I can't, sir,' the sick man said, 'for I have no one to put me into the pool when the water bubbles up. Someone else always*

gets there ahead of me.' Jesus told him, 'Stand up, pick up your mat, and walk!' Instantly, the man was healed! He rolled up his sleeping mat and began walking! But this miracle happened on the Sabbath, so the Jewish leaders objected. They said to the man who was cured, 'You can't work on the Sabbath! The law doesn't allow you to carry that sleeping mat!' But he replied, 'The man who healed me told me, "Pick up your mat and walk."' 'Who said such a thing as that?' They demanded. The man didn't know, for Jesus had disappeared into the crowd. But afterward Jesus found him in the Temple and told him, 'Now you are well; so stop sinning, or something even worse may happen to you.' Then the man went and told the Jewish leaders that it was Jesus who had healed him."
(John 5:1-15)

In this story, multitudes came to the pool of Bethesda seeking the grace of the Greek god of healing, hoping to find relief from their sicknesses and diseases. What's interesting about this particular story is that Jesus came to the pool. This was not a place where the people were gathered to worship Him or to hear Him speak about the Kingdom of God. This was a place where desperate people with serious problems came to seek a mythical god that could not help them. Jesus entered this shrine of idol worship to intervene.

This particular man had wasted 38 years of his life, hanging all his hopes and dreams on an idol who could not heal him. Fortunately, for him, Jesus of Nazareth, whom Christians call the "Great Physician," would seek him out on this particular day and prove what I am asserting here: God can do what medical science cannot. Thirty-eight years of suffering were about to end. Thirty-eight years of limitation were about to be interrupted. Thirty-eight years of sorrow and pain were about to be confronted by the Great Physician for someone who had spent his life seeking the answers of an idol of healing. In one encounter, Jesus would change the course of this man's life. He would give him meaning. He would give him hope. Hope is the anchor of the soul.

Before Jesus intervened, He asked this lame man a question. "Do you want to be well?" Any ordinary person would immediately and emphatically answer in the affirmative, wouldn't they? Jesus was asking more than that, though. He was good at asking loaded questions, and He never asked a question to which He didn't already know the answer. The deeper question was, "Are you willing to embrace the process?" The implications of that question are much more complicated. Embracing the process of healing would require the man at the pool to change his focus, his direction, his thought processes, and his priorities. He could not continue doing what he'd done for 38 years. He could not stay where he had been for 38 years. When Jesus asked, "Do you want to be well?" He was asking, "Are you ready to embrace the process of your healing?" You may be thinking, "Wait a minute. This was an instantaneous, miraculous healing. The man didn't have to do anything. What was the process?"

The process of healing from emotional pain must address the lies they propagate.

The number one lie of anxiety and depression is the one that affects our relationship with self: I can't. In reply to Jesus' question, the lame man offered an excuse. "I can't..." He had been saying "I can't" for 38 years. I can't get up. I can't get my legs to work. I can't muster the courage to try. I can't get anyone to help me. I can't get failure out of my mind. I can't feel anything anymore. I can't trust myself. I can't change my reputation. I can't regain the time I've lost.[86] The man at the pool had an "I can't" mentality. The first step of his process was to overcome this mentality.

Oh, but he had a backup excuse. Have you ever had a backup excuse? As a parent, one of my pet peeves is when one of my children begins a statement with "But…" It means an excuse is coming. And if the first one doesn't work, there's always a backup. Notice his backup excuse: "I have no one to put me into the pool when the water is stirred. Someone else always gets there ahead of me." Not only did he have an "I can't" mentality, but he had a "they won't" mentality. This is just another lie of anxiety and depression; this lie affects our relationship with others. They won't help me. They won't carry me. They won't give me a chance. They won't believe in me. They won't pray for me. They won't forget my past. They won't look beyond my infirmity. They won't love me. They won't forgive me. The two greatest obstacles he had to overcome, as part of his process, were these two crushing mentalities.

Personally, the Devil often uses these two excuses as an indictment against me to subvert me from my mission. "I can't do what I'm called to do. I can't reach the goals that I've set for myself. I can't pursue my destiny. I can't rise above my own self-condemnation. I can't overcome my fear. I can't forgive myself for what has happened. I can't, I can't, I can't." You've been there, haven't you? You wake up in the morning, already struggling with the echo of "I can't" in your mind. You go to bed at night wrestling to sleep because you can't stop the sound of "I can't" in your spirit.

And if you manage to get free from that, the enemy will begin using the backup, "they won't." "Even if you could reach that goal, they won't help you. Even if you could overcome your fear, they won't support you. Even if you could forgive yourself, they won't give you a chance. Even if you could accomplish that difficult feat, they won't believe in you. They won't forget your past. They won't pray for you. They won't look beyond your faults. They won't, they won't, they won't!"

The process requires the silencing of these two lies: "I can't" and "they won't." The truth is, you can and they will!

So what does this man's story have to do with anxiety and depression? Imagine you had spent 38 years as an invalid, lying down like a beggar in a place where you would never find help. The psychological damage this must've caused would be near catastrophic. You and I have suffered unbearable intangible pain over much less suffering than this man with no use of his legs. Physical sickness is a proven trigger of depression; he could've been the poster child of his day.

To interject some personal context, as a police officer, I was an investigator of crime. As a minister, I'm an investigator of scripture. I like to think that being good at one makes me better at the other. Attempting to read this crippled man's mind (as I did above) is as easy as listening carefully to what comes out of his mouth and putting it into personal context. I can compare his words with my own thoughts and experiences and find a point of commonality. For instance, I've never been without the use of my legs, but I have often felt like I wasn't as capable as others. My success has never been held back by physical infirmity, but I have felt held back by my own self-limiting beliefs. Going through this identification exercise as I read through the story helps me get a glimpse of what his life might have looked like.

I believe this lame man's mind was just as crippled as his legs. He overcame the crippling mentality with action. Jesus prescribed his healing process in three clear and concise steps. He said, "Stand up, pick up your mat, and walk." That's it. That was the process. Those were the instructions. Jesus' healing miracles always came with specific instructions.

Let's examine the three steps.

Step one. Stand up. In those first two little words of instruction, the lame man would have to act against everything he had known and experienced for the past 38 years. He had not had use of his legs or feet for 38 years. He had been laying on the ground on a mat. Any mobility, any movement, any change in his situation, his surroundings, or his atmosphere had required him to lean upon someone else. To stand up meant that he would have to trust his legs. They haven't been trustworthy for 38 years. Perhaps he had tried to stand up many times before thinking, "Maybe today is my day." Maybe he had tried to get to the pool on his own, but the moment he would place the minutest amount of trust in his legs, they would fail him as before.

To stand up meant to do what he's never been able to do before. What does "stand up" mean to you? What does that require of you? What will you have to do that you've never been able to do before? Who will you have to trust that you've never been able to trust before? What will you have to try that you have tried but failed before? Stand up, stop being the victim, and do what no one believes you can do.

This was a mental process just as much as a physical one. When Seth was having an anxiety attack, it would've been futile (and insulting) for me to say to him, "Everything's fine. Calm down." That wouldn't have helped him at all. It may even have made things worse! Two people you should never ask to calm down are your wife and someone having an anxiety attack! I can hear Jesus saying to this poor man, "Just get up," as if it were as easy as one, two, three.

Step two. Jesus instructed him, "Pick up your mat." The second step of the process was to let go of his security blanket. The mat had a purpose. Its purpose was to give him a softer place to lay—to help him cope with his limitations. The mat made the pain just a little bit easier to manage. The mat's purpose, however, would be negated by the man's healing.

Sometimes we struggle to let go of things that once had a purpose in our lives. What had a purpose in one season, could be the thing that holds you back in another season. Sometimes that means letting go of people. As harsh as it sounds, people will let you know when it's time to let them go if you pay attention.

"Pick up your mat" means to stop using unhealthy coping mechanisms to get through the day. Stop self-medicating. Stop turning to the things to which you're holding on to help you survive. You will no longer need your mat. You will no longer need something to help you cope. Your crutches are no longer necessary. Your walls are no longer necessary. Your defense mechanisms are not going to be needed. Pick up your mat. As long as the mat is there, you will be tempted to use it to continue living with and getting used to your infirmity.

The interesting thing about your "mat" is that it has always been there for you. It's easy, it's readily available. There will always be something there to medicate your discomfort. There will always people there to enable you. It's easier to use your mat instead of motivating yourself to stand up and walk in your healing. It's easier to trust in the things that are familiar than it is to set out on the journey of being healed. The man at the pool laid on his mat for 38 years; it's all he knew. It was comfortable, it was familiar, and it was trustworthy, but it was the one thing that he would no longer need.

Pick up your mat. Stop using the mat as your excuse. Stop blaming your upbringing. Stop blaming your atmosphere. Stop blaming your lack of opportunity. Stop blaming it on others' unwillingness to help you, and pick up your mat!

Step three. The third and final instruction Jesus gave him was one word. "Walk." Verse 9 says, "Instantly, the man was healed! He rolled up his sleeping mat and began walking!" Notice, the healing had already taken place, but he still had to complete the process. The healing took place somewhere between getting up and picking up his mat; however, the process wouldn't be complete until he walked. He was already healed, he was already able, but the process that he was responsible for wouldn't be complete until he walked.

You see, the process isn't for God; it's for you. Instantly, the man was healed, but he hadn't gone anywhere. You can be healed and still not embrace your change. You can be healed and still not make progress. You can be healed and still not realize you are until you finish your process.

Your healing may involve therapy, medication, a change in behavior, or any number of things, but it will always require Jesus to be in the equation. Where science can't, Jesus can.

Case 2: The Arthritic

In the 13th chapter of the Gospel of Luke, we are introduced to a woman who is described as "bent over" by a "spirit of weakness." Her age is unknown, but she has suffered from this condition for eighteen years. Dr. John Wilkinson, a medical missionary and expert on the healing miracles of Jesus, conducted a study of her condition based on the original text of Luke's Gospel. He suggests that she has a disease called Ankylosing spondylitis, a type of arthritis causing her vertebrae to become inflamed and fused which, after eighteen years, resulted in a "bent over" posture. The onset of the disease can begin in early adulthood and be accompanied by chronic pain.[87] [88] This unnamed woman is not able to stand up straight; however, her presence in the synagogue on the Sabbath day suggests that she is mobile, functional, and trying to carry out a normal life despite her probable discomfort.

> "On a Sabbath Jesus was teaching in one of the synagogues, and a woman was there who had been crippled by a spirit for eighteen years. She was bent over and could not straighten up at all. When Jesus saw her, he called her forward and said to her, "Woman, you are set free from your infirmity."

Then he put his hands on her, and immediately she straightened up and praised God." (Luke 13:10-13 NIV)

Jesus, the Great Physician, met another woman who had suffered for a great length of time. Eighteen years to be precise. When you suffer from something for that long, it becomes normal. Nothing Jesus ever did or does was or is normal. Most Kings were born in a palace; Jesus was born in a stable. Most kings were the lineage of royalty; Jesus was just a carpenter's son. Most kings possess earthly riches; Jesus had no place to lay His head. Nothing Jesus said was ever normal. He said if you want to be great, be a servant. If you want to be first, be last. If you want to have wealth, give away everything you have. Nothing about Jesus or his kingdom was or is or ever will be *normal.* Jesus was always drawn to people with pain like the woman he met in the synagogue one Sabbath day.

This unnamed woman had been crippled by a spirit for eighteen years. It was just a normal Sabbath day, Jesus was teaching in a synagogue as usual, and this woman was present. Perhaps it was a normal day for her, but her normal was unlike others. It was full of difficulty. She was bent over, and couldn't straighten up at all. She must've had difficulty walking, difficulty sitting, difficulty carrying water from the well, difficulty going about her daily life. I can't imagine that anything about her life was easy.

For eighteen years, this woman's perspective had not changed. Think about that number for a moment. It's the period of time between when you are born and when you are considered an adult. It's the period of time you have to equip your children with the tools necessary to be successful in life. Now, imagine spending all that time bent over, unable to straighten up, unable to see where you're going, unable to live a normal life.

She was crippled by a spirit. The original Greek word for "spirit" is *pneuma*. It's the root word of pneumonia. It means wind or breath. She had a spirit of Satan breathing upon her, causing her to be bent over. A study of biblical numerology shows us that the number eighteen is significant because it represents bondage.[89] This was eighteen years of bondage this woman was never going to get back. But for her, it had become normal. What may seem like a miserable existence for you and me was normal for her. What you and I might consider humiliating was normal for her. What you and I might never have been able to cope with was just another normal day for her.

Maybe you can identify with this bent-over woman. Have your anxiety and depression filtered your perspective for so long that it has defined your normal? Have you been living with your brokenness, living with your betrayal, living with your abuse, living with your depression, living with your baggage, and living with your issues for so long that they have become routine? Do you realize that when something has become your normal, it's because you have accepted it? When you accept intangible pain as normal, you have conformed to a new standard. You've accepted that you will always be a failure, you're always going to struggle, you're always going to be in pain. Whatever has you bent over, you've accepted that it will always be that way. "It is what it is."

When you lower your standard of living to accommodate your anxiety, depression, and intangible pain, you will reject the advice and wisdom of people you trust, you won't let people love you, you'll stop taking care of yourself, you'll lose your capacity to trust people, and you will lose your perspective because you are *bent over*.

What this crippled woman must be cognizant of is that everyone can see her pain. What if everyone around you could see your pain? The very thought of that probably makes you want to slide down in your easy chair, right? You've accepted it, but you don't want anybody to see it. That's why you still put on your proverbial mask, greet everybody with a smile, and tell them you're doing fine—because you don't want anybody to see you're struggling! If someone else got a look at your normal, it would shock them. They might look at you differently. They might shy away from you. Or maybe they would try to fix you. We don't want anybody to see what we have accepted as normal. It's amazing what people will live with just because they have become comfortable with it.

From an outside perspective, one might've looked upon this bent-over woman and said, "What a waste." Eighteen years of her life have been wasted. I want to encourage you: The time you've spent battling anxiety and depression is not wasted time.

I can hear her say, "Wait a minute. Don't call the eighteen years I've spent in this bent-over position a waste of time. You don't know what the Lord taught me. I learned how to survive. I learned what I was capable of. I learned what I was made of. I learned how to do new things. I learned how to adapt, I learned a new way of walking. Even bent over I can still survive."

Let's stop and let this woman testify for a moment:

"I'm bent over, but it hasn't held me back. I'm bent over but I'm still here. I've been bent over with disappointment, bent over with failure, bent over with despair, bent over with fear, bent over with circumstances, bent over with tragedy, but it wasn't a waste. Being bent over taught me how to pray, it increased my faith, it taught me God's faithfulness. I was bent over when he gave me purpose. I was bent over when he gave me dreams and visions. Being bent over made me who I am."

On this day, however, she would encounter the Great Physician who would change her perspective. He noticed her, called her forward, and said, "Woman you are free from your infirmity." Then He reached out and touched her and immediately she straightened up and praise God. I believe the touch was meant to prompt her to look up—to try on her new perspective.

Psychologists say that it takes 21 days to form a habit and 66 days for something to become automatic. Being bent over has been automatic for eighteen years. Perhaps she was so programmed to be bent over, Jesus had to touch her to remind her to look up and stand up. Maybe He touched her chin to get her to raise her head. Maybe He took her by the shoulders and physically lifted her up, showing her that she was healed. The touch of Jesus was to break the automatic and monotonous and show her what her new normal looked like.

It's not that people don't want to be healed, it's not that they don't believe they *can* be healed; it's that they are still in bondage to what has become automatic. This woman would have to learn a new way to walk, talk, and function. This miracle has changed her—not only changed her perspective but also her appearance. Until now, this woman has been recognized for her problem. But now, people will see her at the synagogue next Sunday and say, "Who in the world is this? I've never seen this person before." Jesus gave her a new normal.

Case 3: The Hemophiliac and the Fever

In the Gospel of Luke, chapter eight, we are introduced to a man named Jairus. He was a person of position and prominence; a synagogue ruler, a Pharisee. Historically, Pharisees didn't have a very high opinion of Jesus. Jairus was agonizing over his twelve-year-old daughter, whom the scripture said was dying. He had heard Jesus' teaching in the synagogue and seen one of His miracles. Therefore, he was seeking out Jesus to come to his house and heal his daughter. We do not know her specific sickness, only that it was so severe that she was expected to die. This expectation is supported by the presence of the mourners already at his house when he returned with Jesus.

In the same chapter, we are also introduced to an unnamed woman who had an "issue of blood." There is much speculation about her specific disease, but it is widely believed that she has a female problem that caused uncontrolled bleeding. According to Mosaic law, she is considered unclean. Any place or person she touches is also considered unclean. We do not know her age, but the scripture tells us she suffered from this bleeding for twelve years. She spent all of her resources seeking healing from doctors but did not get any better. She also heard about Jesus' miracles. She reasons within herself that if she can just touch the skirt of his garment, she will be healed.

> *"As Jesus was on his way, the crowds almost crushed him. And a woman was there who had been subject to bleeding for twelve years, but no one could heal her. She came up behind him and touched the edge of his cloak, and immediately her bleeding stopped. 'Who touched me?' Jesus asked. When they all denied it, Peter said, 'Master, the people are crowding and pressing against you.' But Jesus said, 'Someone touched me; I know that power has gone out from me.' Then the woman, seeing that she could not go unnoticed, came trembling and fell at his feet. In the presence of all the people, she told why she had touched him and how she had been instantly healed. Then he said to her, 'Daughter, your faith has healed you. Go in peace.' While Jesus was still speaking, someone came from the house of Jairus, the synagogue*

leader. 'Your daughter is dead,' he said. 'Don't bother the teacher anymore.' Hearing this, Jesus said to Jairus, 'Don't be afraid; just believe, and she will be healed.'" (Luke 8:42-50 NIV)

When little girls are laying on their deathbed, their fathers don't leave their bedside. Jairus was probably no different if it weren't for one thing: Jesus was near. The beloved teacher, the one who had performed miracles in the synagogue, was the only one who could stop the death of his daughter. For that hope, Jairus left his daughter's bedside to go get Jesus.

When he found Jesus, he fell at His feet and pleaded with him to come to his house and heal his twelve-year-old daughter. There was no hesitation, no further dialogue between them recorded in scripture. The next phrase in Luke 8:42 is, "As Jesus was on His way..." Everything was going to be okay. Jairus must've been relieved.

Twelve years earlier, about the same time that little girl was born, there was a woman who started getting sick. She started bleeding and couldn't get it to stop. Over the next several years, she would spend all her resources trying to find a doctor that could help her but to no avail. According to religious laws of her time, her bleeding made her unclean and subject to the same societal restrictions as those with diseases like leprosy. She had to keep her distance, live outside the city, and wear the societal label of rejection.

Fast forward twelve years. Like many, she had heard about the Rabbi that had been teaching in the synagogue who had the power to heal. She had heard stories of lame men walking and blind men seeing—miracles attributed to this man called the Son of God. Because Jesus could rarely go anywhere without drawing a crowd, it would've been difficult for this sick woman to miss Jesus' visit to her town. She blended into the crowd, trying to get a glimpse of Jesus, hoping against hope that He might heal her, too. She said within herself, "If I can just touch the hem of his robe, I know I will be made clean."

She crawled through the crowd, hoping no one would recognize her as the unclean woman who lived outside the city. She worked her way closer to her miracle, inch by inch through dust and the dung of animals, until she found herself at the feet of Jesus. She looked up and saw that Jesus was talking to a synagogue ruler. The man was upset; something about his little girl being sick. He was motioning for Jesus to follow him. "Oh no!" She must've thought, "I'm going to miss my opportunity! The Rabbi is leaving!" All at once, she stretched her arm out as far as she could and grabbed the edge of Jesus' robe for just a second.

She was immediately healed. It must've felt like a wave of heat going through her body, for the Scripture says Jesus felt virtue go out of him. In a moment, her disease was gone. With it went the uncleanness, rejection, disgrace, and humiliation. Her separation was over. Her limitations were removed. Her pain was gone. She had hope for a new future. She would have opportunities she never had. Everything about her life would be different from here.

The miracle stopped Jesus in His tracks. He turned around and said, "Who touched my clothes?" One person's miracle became another person's interruption.

This was an unusual question because Jesus was surrounded by people, many of whom were pressing against him trying to get closer. One of his disciples pointed out his ridiculous question, but He persisted because there was an impartation of power. Jesus didn't want to continue on without acknowledging the healing. His acknowledgment would fulfill her legal responsibility to be declared clean by a priest.

It would also be a public reaffirmation of her acceptance and worthiness. Jesus vouched for her in front of the whole city.

Jesus said to her, "Daughter, your faith has healed you." After twelve years of suffering, spending all her money on physicians, and getting no better, her sickness was finally healed. The evidence of her miracle was her faith.

Meanwhile, Jairus is still standing, watching this unfold. He still needs Jesus to come to his house. His daughter still needs a miracle. Minutes matter. Perhaps even seconds. But Jesus has been interrupted by this unclean woman. What is he doing? No! Don't stop! We have to go. My daughter is dying!

Before Jesus could turn back toward Jairus, someone came from his house and said, "There's no need for the Master to come, your daughter is already dead." Jesus stopped him and said, "Don't be afraid, just believe, and your daughter will be healed." After pointing to the evidence of the woman's faith, Jesus reassured Jairus that his faith was evidence enough of his daughter's healing!

Case Closed

In all three cases, the afflicted person had suffered for a long period of time (38 years, 18 years, and 12 years). In all three cases, Jesus conducted an intervention, a *divine* intervention. In all three cases, instant miraculous healing occurred. These healing stories are evidence: the testimony of a reliable, credible, and faithful God. He has never been rebutted, refuted, or repudiated. Case closed.

> *"God is not a man, so he does not lie. He is not human, so he does not change his mind. Has he ever spoken and failed to act? Has he ever promised and not carried it through?" (Numbers 29:13)*

CHAPTER 7

Challenging the Lies

We are, in fact, body, mind (soul), and spirit. The scripture makes that distinction.

> *"May God himself, the God who makes everything holy and whole, make you holy and whole, put you together—spirit, soul, and body—and keep you fit for the coming of our Master, Jesus Christ. The One who called you is completely dependable. If he said it, he'll do it!"* (1 Thessalonians 5:23 MSG)

Therefore, any definition of healing must include body, soul, and spirit. Jesus illustrated this when He healed a woman he met at a well in the Gospel of John. This encounter doesn't really qualify as a miracle in terms of divine healing because the woman was not seeking relief from a physical illness. But it is a miracle because she was healed from emotional and intangible pain. This miracle paints a beautiful portrait of the way Jesus ministers to the whole person by peeling away multiple layers of pain.

The woman in the story (depicted in John 4) is a Samaritan. She was not ordinary. She was carrying the baggage of years of emotional pain. She was a woman of ill repute, a woman with a reputation, a woman with a record, a woman whose name was often used in vain. She had an affliction that was not physical but affected every area of her life. She needed healing emotionally, mentally, and spiritually. This unnamed woman knew rejection. She knew shame. She knew isolation. She knew resentment. She no longer believed in herself and, certainly, no longer believed in others. She had never had a meaningful relationship. This Samaritan woman was suffering from *soul sickness.*

Like many, she suffered layer upon layer of suppressed emotional pain. Little did she know that a Jewish man named Jesus was coming through town, would meet her at the town well, and would walk her through the healing process. The story explains how Jesus peeled away each layer of her heartache to set her free. Undoubtedly, you will see yourself in this woman's experience. Here's a brief introduction to the story.

> *"Soon a Samaritan woman came to draw water, and Jesus said to her, 'Please give me a drink.' He was alone at the time because his disciples had gone into the village to buy some food. The woman was surprised, for Jews refuse to have anything to do with Samaritans. She said to Jesus, 'You are a Jew, and I am a Samaritan woman. Why are you asking me for a drink?' Jesus replied, 'If you only knew the gift God has for you and who you are speaking to, you would ask me, and I would give you living water.'"* (John 4:7-10)

The Layer of Self-Belief

Henry Ford believed one's success is closely tied to one's belief in oneself. Your self-belief or self-efficacy is formed over your lifetime by several factors. The four main sources of self-belief are: (1) being successful, (2) having successful role models, (3) receiving affirmation, and (4) being emotionally, mentally, and physically healthy.[90]

This poor woman is zero for four. Her interaction with Jesus bears this out. Jesus came through Samaria and, tired from the journey, sat down by Jacob's well in the village of Sychar around noon. The woman in question came to the well and encountered Jesus who asked her, "Would you give me a drink?" Her reply revealed her self-belief.

To paraphrase, she said, "I'm a Samaritan and you're a Jew. There are cultural differences between us. Jews do not associate with Gentiles. You shouldn't even be speaking to me because I'm not worthy. Your people look down upon my people. They call us 'dogs' We're not even permitted to eat from the same dishes because we're perceived to be unclean."

Her emotional wounds were buried under a layer of negative self-belief. Because she was a Samaritan, she believed she was not worthy to have a conversation with Jesus, a Jew. Many people shun the healing process because their negative self-belief holds them back—as if they must reach a certain standard before being eligible to get well. If you don't believe you are good enough, worthy enough, successful enough, intelligent enough, or "whatever" enough to be healed, you most likely won't be.

The Scripture gives us no history of this woman other than when seen in the above passage. She may not have ever been successful. She may have never had a positive or successful role model. She may have never received affirmation from anyone important in her life. She certainly wasn't well mentally or emotionally. This layer of negative self-belief stood in the way of her well-being. It will stand in your way, as well.

You must address the layer of self-belief. The words, events, and emotions that created that negative self-belief have to be challenged. Jesus did that with His Word. It's going to bear a resemblance to ripping the bandage off an untreated wound. It'll hurt, but it'll heal.

The Layer of Logic

This was Jesus' reply:

"If you only knew the gift God has for you and who you are speaking to, you would ask me, and I would give you living water." (John 4:10)

The Samaritan woman isn't getting it. She hears what Jesus is saying, but she is listening with her head instead of her heart. She says, "But sir, how can you draw water for me? You don't have anything to draw with and the well is too deep." Logically, Jesus' words didn't make sense to her. Logic said it was impossible for Jesus to give her something to drink because He did have a rope and a bucket. If she had been listening with her heart, she would've understood that Jesus was talking about water that didn't require a rope and bucket to draw with. Her heart was broken, but her head was looking for more answers.

Isn't it frustrating when our minds talk us out of what our hearts want to embrace? This is the emergence of the lies of anxiety and depression. "Jesus, this is impossible. It doesn't make any sense. There is no logic in this. How can you give me water? How can I be healed? How can you restore the brokenness in my life? How can you fix something so broken? I don't even know how it got so broken!"

What God wants to do in your life may not make sense. It may not pass the logic test. Don't miss your moment because your mind couldn't find the logic in it. Peel away the layer of logic. It'll stifle your faith and steal your hope. Remember, hope is the anchor of the soul!

Jesus persisted, "Those who drink the water I give will never be thirsty again." Her response was still coming from the layer of her logic, perhaps laced with a bit of sarcasm. She said, "Give me some of this water so that I will not have to keep coming to the well to draw." This wasn't a battle of wits, it was a battle between the flesh and the Spirit. Jesus was penetrating through the layers of her pain. She was still hiding behind the first layer, but Jesus was ten steps ahead of her in the conversation.

What he said next bypassed logic and went straight to the heart of the matter. The woman wasn't expecting what He would say next. He called her out. He rang her bell. He read her mail. Everybody needs somebody that isn't afraid to dispense with the niceties, cut through the noise, and confront their issues.

"Go get your husband and bring him here." Jesus forced the woman to confront the truth, once and for all, exposing her wound for the sake of healing. This brings us to the next layer.

The Layer of Denial

The woman replied, "I don't have a husband." She was covering her wounds with a layer of denial. Oh, she was telling the truth, or at least her version of it, but she was ignoring the reality of her truth. The fact was, as Jesus would point out in his reply, she had five husbands and the man she was living with was not her husband. She didn't yet know she was speaking to the Messiah and that he was about to ring her bell. Again.

Denial and suppression are common defense mechanisms. Both are methods of blocking harmful events and thoughts from the conscious mind without a change of the situation that is producing them. This is accomplished by twisting the reality of that situation in some way.[91] That the woman was exhibiting these defenses is proof she was struggling with severe emotional pain. Nobody survives five failed marriages unscathed. Regardless of who was at fault in these broken relationships, she had to be carrying serious baggage. Perhaps she had suffered the damage of betrayal, rejection, or abuse. Perhaps five emotional tragedies were all she could handle, and she therefore resorted to a cheap and disposable self-belief. Either way, she was defending her mind by blocking out years of trauma.

Defense mechanisms ultimately make things worse. Suppressed feelings, emotions, or intrusive thoughts eventually have to manifest in some way. If left untreated, they can contribute to stress, anxiety, depression, and even physical problems like heart disease.[92]

Jesus forced the Samaritan woman to confront what she had hidden from herself and others. His message to her was, "You don't have to put on a mask anymore. You don't have to hide the pain. You don't have to spend another day wrestling with the shame and guilt you've been carrying. I already know what you did. I know your history. Lower your defenses. Today, you're going to be free."

The Layer of False Belief

Have you noticed, every time Jesus speaks to the woman, she has a deflecting response? Every time He peels away one of the layers of her pain, it reveals another layer. She's not trying to out-smart Him; she has just hurt for so long that the layers of pain seem like the rings of a tree trunk. Pain produces more pain.

Jesus saw through the layers and was connecting with her on a deeper level. When He brought up her five husbands and current boyfriend, she quickly produced a deflecting response. She didn't seem to be shaken by Jesus' words but saw them as another opportunity to divert the subject away from her issues.

"Your people say that we should worship in the temple, our fathers say we should worship in the mountains." The Samaritan woman didn't want to talk about her husbands, so she turned to doctrine instead. Jesus wasn't there to discuss doctrine and squashed the subject by telling her that *how* she worshipped was more important than *where* she worshipped.

Let's deal with the layer of false belief. To put it plainly, some aren't able to walk the healing process because false belief (or doctrine) has a stronghold in their lives. I'm not talking about heresy. I'm talking about someone who loves the Lord, is sincere in his or her beliefs, but has been taught something that has no scriptural basis by someone they trusted.

Let me explain. When I was twenty-one years old, I was faced with the first of many personal tragedies. My first daughter, Kailei Elizabeth, was born with two major heart defects. For ten weeks, we prayed for her. We had fasted for her healing. We believed God was going to bring her through it. Her surgeon said she had an 80% chance of survival. She died in open-heart surgery at Vanderbilt University Medical Center in Nashville on April 10, 1996.

In the wake of that tragedy, someone made a statement to me that I struggled with for many years. There was a woman in the church whom I believed to be a Godly woman and whom I believed knew how to pray and was very biblically sound. This woman came to me and said, "I'm very sorry for your loss, but I feel I have to tell you that if you had more faith your daughter would still be alive." Put yourself in my position and let that image sink in for a moment. Even if she was right, who says something like that to a twenty-one-year-old father who just buried his child?

First of all, there is not a word in all of Scripture to support what that woman said to me. Secondly, it scarred me. I struggled with that for years. The devil used those words to plant a seed of guilt in my life. I went through a season in which I believed it was my fault my daughter had not survived. That lie followed me through the death of my little brother three years later. Twenty-one years later, that lie would follow me into a hospital room at Cleveland Clinic where my Dad breathed his last breath. This was my first-hand experience with religious doubt or struggle that we discussed in chapter 5.

I knew the moment those words came out of that woman's mouth, it was false doctrine. I knew that God didn't take my child's life as punishment for some sort of lack of faith. My heart knew, but my head struggled for years. That layer of false belief caused me great damage.

Perhaps, you have had a similar experience with false belief. Don't let it distract you from your healing process. Go to God's Word and let him teach you, challenging the false belief with the truth. This is what the scripture says about that:

> *"I've written to warn you about those who are trying to deceive you. But they're no match for what is embedded deeply within you—Christ's anointing, no less! You don't need any of their so-called teaching. Christ's anointing teaches you the truth on everything you need to know about yourself and him, uncontaminated by a single lie. Live deeply in what you were taught." (2 John 2:26-27 MSG)*

The Layer of Perception

Finally, the Samaritan woman had to peel back the layer of perception. She said, "the Messiah is coming. And he's going to explain it all to us." She did not have the discernment to realize the Messiah was standing right in front of her, explaining everything to her! How many times have we missed an opportunity because we were waiting for the opportunity to come in a different package, or from a different direction?

The eyes of her understanding were opened when Jesus revealed himself to her. This is one of the things I love about God. He's always at work in our situation long before we recognize His presence. That's because we interpret what we see and hear through the filter of experience. Every past experience she had with men was one of dysfunction. She had no precedent by which to properly judge Jesus' intentions. He had to introduce himself to cut through the layers of her distorted perception.

When that last layer was finally peeled off, something powerful happened. The Samaritan woman's focus immediately shifted from her pain to her purpose; from her mess to her Messiah. Suddenly she had a message, and she didn't waste any time telling it. She ran into town, grabbed anyone who would listen, and said, "Come and see! Come and see a man who's told me everything that I have ever done! Could this be the Messiah?"

Why does it hurt to heal? Because the healing process requires the layers to be peeled away. Ultimately, the healing will create a scar where the wound used to be. And the scar won't hurt anymore. The scar will not get infected, the scar will not fester, the scar will not break open. The scar is there for a reminder. God healed this. This used to be a wound. This used to be a matter of contention in my life. This used to be something that I couldn't talk about. This used to be something that I denied and couldn't face, and it just kept getting worse. This used to be something that held me back, that hindered me from reaching my destiny. This used to be the thing that cast doubt over my life, but now it's healed. The Lord has restored it. The scar is there to remind you of the goodness and faithfulness of God. It hurts to heal. But don't be afraid of the healing process. Don't be afraid to expose the wound. For therein is God glorified.

CHAPTER 8

It Wasn't Supposed to Happen to Me

E xposing your wound is painful because it requires you to acknowledge what happened. We have difficulty with that acknowledgment because we are likely among those that have said, "It will never happen to me." We say it, either out of self-righteousness or genuine resolve, never imagining we would one day find ourselves in a place we so abhorred. We defensively go from saying "It will never happen to me" to "It wasn't *supposed* to happen to me."

I wasn't supposed to lose my job. I wasn't supposed to get abused. I wasn't supposed to lose my child. I wasn't supposed to go through bankruptcy. I wasn't supposed to receive that diagnosis. I wasn't supposed to go through a divorce. I wasn't supposed to get addicted. *It* wasn't supposed to happen to me. What is your *it*? What is that thing you can't escape, that causes pain, regret, or even shame and embarrassment? What is it that wasn't supposed to happen to you?

It is not supposed to become your identity. *It* is not supposed to define the rest of your life. *It* is not what or who you are destined to be. *It* does not have to have power over you. *It* does not cancel your purpose, plans, or dreams. *It* is up to you. How you choose to react to *it* will determine the role *it* plays in the rest of your life.

It will either become your excuse or it will become your purpose. Listen to the difference.

It wounded me. I'm lonely because *it* happened. *It* made me an angry person. I lost time and/or money because *it* happened. *It* cost me my credibility. I can't forgive myself because *it* happened. *It* took away my ability to trust. I can't sleep at night because *it* happened. *It* made me suicidal. This is what your conversations sound like when your pain has become your excuse. If you let *it* become your excuse for failure, you'll spend the rest of your life pointing your finger at something or someone else. You will repel relationships and opportunities. The thing that you use to excuse your deficits will define your legacy.

You can expect that those clinging to an excuse aren't looking for healing or purpose. They will be stuck for the rest of their lives at the very moment of their affliction. They will never get past their pain. They will never forgive. They will never become more mature. They will never learn anything from what they've been through. While they have burned everything down around them and are laying there on a pile of life's ashes, hurting people are pleading, "Show me how to get up! Show me how to make it through this! Somebody, please help me!"

Instead, make a conscious decision to make *it* your purpose in life. When your pain transforms your purpose, your speech will attract an audience. When people hear you say things like "Don't let *it* wound you" or "Don't allow *it* to steal your joy," they will be attracted to you. People are attracted to people who talk about answers, who tell others how they turned *it* around! Answers give you a platform.

It's easy to recognize someone who lives a life of purpose

birthed from their pain. Just listen to their conversations. "Let me tell you how I overcame loneliness. Let me tell you how the Lord restored the time I lost. Let me tell you how I regained my credibility. I had a hard time forgiving myself, but this is how I did it. For a long time, I couldn't trust people, but I've reclaimed my faith in others. *It* taught me to fight back. *It* taught me to survive on my own. *It* gave me confidence in myself. *It* showed me what I was really made of. *It* wasn't supposed to happen, but I'm a better person because of what *it* taught me." This is what purpose sounds like.

When *it* happens to you, it gives you compassion for others who had the experience. It teaches you how to give grace because you needed grace. It teaches you how to have patience because you needed someone to be patient with you. That's why the Bible says, "Tribulation works patience" (Romans 5:3 NKJV).

Healthy, happy, successful people are not people who have never failed or suffered pain. They are people who gave purpose to their pain instead of allowing it to define their existence. They said, "*It* wasn't supposed to happen to me, but I'm going to leverage the wisdom I have gained from the experience to improve my life and the lives of others." Success never gives you a platform. Pain gives you a platform. Success is a byproduct of your reaction to pain.

Solving the Puzzle

When I was a kid, I was never really good at puzzles because I got fixated on one piece. Because I don't have a creative mind, I can't see where the piece goes in the bigger picture. I can lay all the pieces out on the table, but no matter how hard I look, I have a difficult time figuring out how all of the individual, different-shaped, and different-colored pieces make a beautiful picture. Figuratively speaking, there was a time I felt this way about life as well. Nothing was making sense. It was difficult, confusing, and discouraging.

Life really is like a puzzle, isn't it? Romans 8:28 gives us a beautiful promise that God is putting that puzzle together:

> *"For we know that all things work together for good to those who love God, to those who are called according to His purpose."*

This puzzle of life with all the pieces, all the seasons, all the events, all the good times and bad, does add up to something beautiful if we can learn to zoom out and see the bigger picture. We experience seasons of plenty, seasons of lack, seasons of sowing and reaping. Look at all of the pieces laid out before you, and hear the Apostle Paul saying, "All of the pieces will fit together for good for those who love God and are called according to His purpose."

What's going on in your life? Maybe you've lost your job. Maybe you are struggling financially. Maybe you don't know where the next meal is coming from. Whatever difficulties you are currently facing, you may be asking, "How can this piece fit anywhere in God's plan for my life?" Sometimes God's plan for us feels like a puzzle because we don't know what the big picture is. Perhaps we've seen the big picture, but as life begins to unfold, we don't see how they could possibly fit in the master plan.

Consider your life and everything that has happened along the way. From A to Z, if you look at things in terms of pieces of a puzzle: every failure, every bad day, every tragedy, every triumph, every success, and every disappointment eventually has to agree with or fit into God's plan for you. Sometimes we misunderstand scripture. Sometimes we read, "All things will work for our good," and we misunderstand it to mean everything that happens to us will be good. That's not what the scripture promises.

If you expect everything that happens to you to be good as a measuring stick for how faithful God is, then you have taken His word out of context, and will go through life wondering where God is. On the contrary, when something bad happens, He can take that thing and can cause it to fit exactly where it belongs in God's plan. All of the puzzle pieces fit together. All things aren't good, but all things fit together or work together for our good. So, don't get discouraged, just zoom out.

In Romans 8:28, the words translated "work together" come from one Greek word *sunergeó*. It means "to cooperate with." I want to show you something in 2 Corinthians 10:5 out of The Message Bible:

> *"We use our powerful God-tools for smashing warped philosophies, tearing down barriers erected against the truth of God, fitting every loose thought and emotion and impulse into the structure of life shaped by Christ. Our tools are ready at hand for clearing the ground of every obstruction and building lives of obedience into maturity."*

When you trust God with the puzzle that is your life, you will find yourself less anxious.

Embrace the Process

You have to decide whether or not you want to be healed.

Healing is the process of becoming sound. To become sound is to become free of injury or disease. Healing is not "being" but "becoming." It's a process: a series of actions or steps to become free of injury or disease. "Embrace the process." Everyone says that. What does it mean? For me, it means making a commitment to move forward one action at a time, one step at a time, one day at a time until "becoming" finally gives way to "being." Once complete, the process is replaced by the product. What is the product of your process? What does your healing look like?

If you are waiting on someone or something to apply the healing process to your life, you're wasting your time. *You* are in charge of your process. It's not going to be imposed upon you. If you are infirm or injured, you have to want healing. Healing doesn't just happen. Healing is sought. You have to take the action or steps necessary to become healed. *You* have to fire the starter pistol. You are in charge of your process, but God is the Healer; He is in charge of the product.

You can't keep saying, "Lord, I trust you to heal me," but then continue to live in the atmosphere that makes you sick. Maybe that's why the Apostle James points out that "Faith by itself isn't enough" (James 2:17). You have to do something. You have to stand up from your bed of affliction, stretch forth your hand, open your eyes, or whatever instructions the Lord has given you, and do what comes next. Embrace your process.

Every healing recorded in scripture had a process. Often, when Jesus performed a miracle it was accompanied by instructions. That's the process. Naaman's process required dipping seven times in the Jordan River. The woman with the issue of blood had to go through the process of crawling on her hands and knees on the dust of the ground through the crowd to touch Jesus. The ten lepers' process required them to go to the temple and show themselves to the priest. The blind man's process required him to wash his eyes.

Everyone's healing has a process. The process, in tandem with the faith of he or she who seeks healing, brings about the product. Everyone's process is different. You can't do someone else's process and get the same product. In the case of the ten lepers, "as they went they were cleansed" (Luke 17:14). Their healing came as they walked out their process.

If you will walk out your process, God will take care of the product. He will heal you!

Many are waiting on their healing as an event. They have prayed, they have taken their place in line, they have "bought their ticket," so to speak, and they're just waiting on the event of their healing to occur. We say things like, "If it's God's will, He will heal me." Frankly, the "if" in that statement negates the purpose of the stripes placed across Jesus' back. It *is* God's will to heal you. The question is: Do you want to be well? If so, you have to understand healing as both a process and an event. The process of your faith moves the hand of God to perform the event of your healing. You are in charge of the process; God is in charge of the event.

In Mark's Gospel, chapter eight, Jesus healed a blind man. This isn't like other miracles recorded in the New Testament. This miracle happened in two stages, and it tends to cause some theological discomfort. Have you noticed we often shy away from passages like this when we don't understand them? The question that begs many answers is, "Why did Jesus open the man's eyes in one stage, then make his sight clear in another?" Couldn't Jesus have touched him once and completed the miracle? Of course, He could have, but that would've bypassed the process.

Look closely at the story:

> *"When they arrived at Bethsaida, some people*
> *brought a blind man to Jesus, and they begged him*
> *to touch the man and heal him. Jesus took the blind*
> *man by the hand and led him out of the village.*
> *Then, spitting on the man's eyes, he laid his hands*
> *on him and asked, 'Can you see anything now?'*
> *The man looked around. 'Yes,' he said, 'I see people,*
> *but I can't see them very clearly. They look like trees*
> *walking around.'" (Mark 8:22-24)*

After reading this passage, the first thing that strikes me is that the blind man's introduction to Jesus was apparently not at his request. The King James Version of verse 22 says "they" brought a blind man to Jesus. Who are they? Maybe the same "they" that are always being quoted. Regardless, "they" were probably just well-meaning folks who wanted to help this poor blind man.

Well-meaning folks are precious. They are folks who want to do something to mitigate your pain and suffering. Sometimes they succeed and sometimes they don't. Sometimes they even make things worse. But, bless their hearts, they are trying.

In this case, two things jump off the pages of the text at me. Firstly, the blind man didn't come to Jesus on his own. Secondly, once he was brought to Jesus, he didn't ask Jesus to heal him. The well-meaning folks that brought him did all the talking. In fact, they begged Jesus to heal him. Being the perceptive Creator of the universe that He is, Jesus must have noticed the blind man was not showing any personal initiative or faith; he was just along for the ride.

I'll be honest, sometimes I don't have the strength to carry myself to the place of encounter. Sometimes I have to get there on the backs of those who are praying for me. There are times I survived only because a praying mother and father were carrying me on their shoulders. I bet you have a similar story. There is no shame in being carried; God sent someone to carrying you when you couldn't get there on your own. Our test begins, however, when we are confronted with the reality that others cannot get us all the way there. God will eventually lead us away from the people and things we've always had to fall back on.

Jesus did not immediately open his eyes. That would've circumvented the process. What Jesus *did* must have, almost immediately, disappointed the man's well-meaning advocates. Jesus took him by the hand. That his eyes weren't immediately opened undoubtedly confused the people. After all, they simply asked Jesus to touch him. Jesus' second action was to lead the man away from the people and take him out of the village. I can almost see the drama play out as people try to figure out what Jesus is doing.

What's happening? Jesus is leading the blind man to walk out his process, leading him to shift his trust away from those who carried him to the place of encounter. Jesus wasn't going to give the blind man new eyes until he separated himself from what he substituted for eyes. Jesus is walking him through the process that will lead him to the product or *event* of his healing. Jesus is ultimately requiring this man with no sight to trust Him exclusively.

There's something else in this story I want to extract. The Bible doesn't tell us this man's name. He is known to us only by his infirmity. This occurs in other places in the scriptures as well, like *the woman with the issue of blood* in Mark 5. When you are suffering, most people identify you by your infirmity. Sometimes that's just as painful as the infirmity itself. It doesn't matter how talented you are, how intelligent you are, how wealthy you are, or what your destiny may be, if you are sick, some people will only know you by your problem. When your name comes up in conversation, these are the people who will say, "Isn't he the one?" or "Isn't she the one?" You have to understand this is not an indication of your character but theirs. If the only way you know me is by my weakness, I don't need you around me.

When I was hurting, I discovered there were people who I thought knew me that stopped knowing me when I fell down. There were people who I considered close friends who passed by on the other side when I needed someone to pour the oil and wine into my wound. You can handle this one of two ways. You can either mourn the loss of those relationships, or you can accept that they were in your life for a season, and your season has changed. You would be surprised how letting certain people go can improve your mental health.

Stop Going Negative

Perspective makes a huge impact on mental health. How you see life can mean the difference between problems and possibilities, between opposition and opportunity. When you see life through the lens of pain, everything looks the same: negative, bland, grey, and dull. Healing will invite you to lift up your head and see life unfiltered.

Some people are just naturally positive and optimistic. I know several people who are that way, and it's easy to like them. Do you have anyone in your life that fits that mold? They are the people who seem to never be upset, anxious, or angry; everything seems to just roll right off of them. It's almost irritating, to be honest. I want to say, "Could you just get mad once in a while, so the rest of us know you're human?"

I'm not one of those people. I confess that I have spent much of my life as a negative person. Having a positive attitude when faced with a challenge is a conscious decision for me. In retrospect, I'm not certain when it began, but I suddenly learned why I'm that way when the phone rang one morning at 5 AM.

At the beginning of the book, I mentioned my daughter and son-in-law were about to have their first baby—my first grandchild. I was nervous about the delivery because of my daughter's struggle with juvenile diabetes. Thankfully, her delivery was without complications and she delivered a healthy baby boy. About a week later, the phone rang at 5 o'clock in the morning. My wife answered and immediately woke me up.

It was my son-in-law. The tone in her voice terrified me when she asked, "What's wrong, Ayden?" I had heard that tone in her voice before in 2017 when we received the call that our nephew had died in his sleep. I had heard that tone in 2018 when she received a call that her brother had been in a car accident that ultimately took his life. I had heard that tone again in 2020 when she received the phone call that her youngest brother had been in a motorcycle accident. For some reason, those calls always seemed to come in the middle of the night or early in the morning. It seemed like an eternity as I waited for her to repeat what Ayden was telling her on the phone. In those few seconds, I had begun to prepare myself to hear that someone was dead.

I am happy to report everyone was eventually fine! My daughter's blood sugar had dropped dangerously low, triggering a 911 call. Although that situation is serious and life-threatening, it's easily corrected. It was then that I realized something. I always go negative because my brain has been trained by so much bad news over the course of my life. Subsequently, when the phone rings at an odd hour, I automatically expect tragic news.

This is an example of neuroplasticity; this is why I go negative. Receiving tragic news on so many occasions over the course of my life has wired my brain to expect it. That's why my brain always goes negative.

So if it's possible for your brain to rewire itself for negativity, does it work the other way around? Absolutely. Neuroplasticity works in a good or bad direction.[93] Rewiring your brain is a daily task. It is your ongoing process.

CHAPTER 9

It Hurts to Heal

I t hurts to heal. That sounds contradictory, doesn't it? The truth of the matter is that there is pain involved in the healing process and that pain is a result of several things that are required when dealing with your pain. Remember, the goal is to turn the wound into a scar. A wound is still bleeding, a wound still hurts, a wound is still unclean, infected, and affects everyday life. But when that wound heals, it turns into a scar that doesn't hurt anymore. It just provides a reminder of your healing and restoration.

My personal experience tells me that pain is inevitable. There's nothing that can be done to avoid pain; it's going to happen. When my son was just a little guy, he was very rambunctious, hyperactive, and accident-prone. Like any little boy, when he became mobile he would come home from daycare just about every day with new bruises, scrapes, and cuts on his limbs. Short of clothing him in a bubble wrap suit, it wasn't preventable. As our children grow older, they begin to learn some of life's hard lessons and, no matter what we do to prepare them, some pain is just inescapable.

I don't know about you, but I believe I didn't really start gaining any wisdom until I crossed the forty-year mark. Of course, when you are in your teens and twenties, you think you know it all. Then, when you reach thirty or forty, you start to realize how ignorant you really were. Time and wisdom have a way of teaching us lessons in which pain was the tutor.

It May Get Worse Before it Gets Better

So, why does the healing process have to hurt? When Seth was seventeen years old, he was no less accident-prone than when he was five. One night, he went to an indoor trampoline park with some of his friends. He was having a great time until he came down on the trampoline and snapped his leg in three places just above the ankle. Thankfully, a police officer was working off-duty security and was able to get EMS there pretty quickly.

Seth called me from the ambulance (keep in mind I didn't yet know what was going on). When I answered, the first thing he said was, "Dad, I'm on morphine." Now, that probably wasn't the best way to lead off that conversation, but I'll give him a little latitude since he was in terrible pain and fighting shock at the sight of a gruesome compound fracture. We laugh about it now, but at that moment, it wasn't what I was expecting to hear. When I asked him to repeat himself, that's when he told me what happened. I remember suddenly being relieved that my son was on morphine. He would experience the most physical pain of his life before it was over.

Why the doctors decided they wouldn't take Seth into surgery until the next morning, I'll never understand. In the meantime, I watched helplessly as my baby boy laid in a hospital bed, writhing in pain, screaming for someone to make it stop. They had splinted and wrapped his leg as best they could, but they couldn't keep his pain under control. The doctor wasn't authorizing enough pain medication to at least make him comfortable and this Dad was getting very upset. I became stern with him until he finally gave my boy something to settle him down. I didn't ever want to hear my son scream like that.

Seth's leg couldn't heal until surgery had been completed to reset the broken bones. After the surgery, he continued to suffer severe pain. My daughter spent that second night in the hospital with him so that we could get some rest. She called in the middle of the night, and as soon as I answered, I could hear Seth screaming in the background as he had before the surgery. The bones were set, the wound was closed and everything was bandaged up, but the trauma to his leg was still causing him unbearable pain. It prompted a very heated exchange with his nurse that finally resulted in something being done to help him.

Seth's leg took months to heal and even longer for his muscles to build back up in that injured leg. He continued experiencing pain, but over time it gradually subsided until it was gone.

The moral of the story is this: As with Seth's injury, sometimes the pain has to get worse before it gets better. Without medical intervention, his broken bones wouldn't have healed, the open wound would have become infected, and he ultimately could have lost his leg. Getting help guaranteed he would eventually heal, but it didn't guarantee the process wouldn't be painful.

Here's the point. Seth wanted to walk again, so he was willing to endure the pain of the process. As much as it hurt, he never once expressed that he didn't want the surgeons to touch his leg. He knew it had to be done because the prognosis of ignoring the injury was devastating compared to the pain of the healing process.

That's the litmus test you have to apply to your pain. Is the pain produced by the healing process worth the product? Or, to use an old euphemism, is the gain worth the pain?

This reminds me of a story I heard somewhere. A man went to see an orthopedic surgeon with a terrible hand injury. He had slammed it in the car door and broken several bones. The surgeon told the man he would need surgery. The man asked, "Will I be able to play the piano after the surgery is over?" The surgeon said, "Yes, after you have healed." The man said, "You must be really good because I've never been able to play the piano!" I suppose that joke should lead into a discussion about misplaced expectations, right? Your expectations going through the healing process certainly have to be realistic. Those expectations will depend on the severity of your wound.

When You Are the Problem

The healing process requires your wound to be exposed. Things that you have suppressed, things that you have blocked out of your mind and heart, things that you don't want to relive will have to be uncovered before they can heal. Sometimes that's the most painful part of the process. Think of it in terms of changing a bandage that has begun to stick to an untreated wound. It's not going to come off easily. It's going to be ugly. It may cause a bit of shock. It may even look much worse than it actually is, but it has to be uncovered before treatment can begin.

Secondly, your wound has to be cleansed. When my brother-in-law had a motorcycle accident and suffered road rash, all the dirt, gravel, and debris that was embedded in the wound had to be cleaned out. When someone suffers severe burns, the dead skin has to be scrubbed off of those burns. It's extremely painful, but it has to be done. The infection has to be cleaned out. It's part of the healing process. You can't delay or skip this step.

Thirdly, bleeding has to be stopped. There has to be a sterile environment. In other words, whatever caused the wound has to be removed from the equation. If the catalyst of your wound is still present, it will repeatedly reopen the wound, causing further pain. You have to get out of the environment that caused the pain for healing to occur.

Wounds of the heart, mind, and emotions are no different than these physical wounds I've used as illustrations. The process of healing is the same.

Sometimes, what stands in the way of your healing is you. What do I mean by that? When I was in the lowest place of my life, I developed crutches, unhealthy coping mechanisms (whatever you want to call them)—things I leaned on and depended on. When I dwelt on my failure, I had an excuse to continue to fail. I had an excuse to be bitter. I had an excuse to be angry. I had an excuse not to succeed and crawl out of the hole I was in. During that season, I didn't want to talk about healing. I wasn't ready. I had learned how to live in pain and had accepted it as my new normal. I knew to seek healing meant to let go of my excuses.

Before you even begin to think about healing, you have to decide you're tired of being bitter—of moaning, groaning, and complaining—and embrace your process. I can tell you from experience, it's worth it. Being able to walk again was worth the pain of the process.

If you are in a low place, using your pain as a justification to stay in bed, be unsuccessful, or even run from God, embracing your healing is worth what you're giving up. Stop allowing your failure to be an excuse to continue failing. Stop allowing your desert season to be an excuse to remain in the desert. You need to heal. You can heal.

Five Kinds of People

Healing invokes a response from people. Many of Jesus miracles elicited a response. Remember the woman who has bent over for eighteen years? When Jesus healed her, it made the temple rulers angry; they stood up in the synagogue and said, "There are six days to work and one for the Sabbath. If you want to be healed, come back on a different day."[94] What about the lame man whom Jesus healed at the pool of Bethesda? When the Jews saw what had happened, they chided the man, "It is the Sabbath; it is not lawful for you to carry your mat on the Sabbath."[95]

This is another one of those lessons learned from experience. There are people who just don't want you to heal. You may think that sounds harsh, but if you look back over your life, you would probably agree there were some who weren't on board with your healing process. Some people want you to continue hurting. Regardless of how twisted it sounds, there are some people who measure their success by your failure and measure their blessing by your misfortune. It's an unfair measurement that puts your issues on the scale opposite theirs, giving themselves an advantage in their own eyes. Identify them and get away from them. Those kinds of relationships stifle the healing process. They'll keep reintroducing the thing that hurt and contaminating the sterile environment required to get well.

Toxic people spread their toxicity. It's like cancer in the body that has to be cut out. Chemotherapy and radiation only mitigate the spread of cancer. Stopping the spread requires an "ectomy": the surgical removal of cancer.[96] Let's face it, there are some relationships in your life you would gladly remove. Then there are others that are more complicated, and emotional ties are not so easily severed. I'm talking about the kind of relationship everyone around you can see is bad for you, but you are blind to it. Your closest friends can tell you how unhealthy the relationship is and you still can't break free. You have to see the cancer for yourself, and until you do, you'll let it keep hurting you.

You need an "ectomy," but it'll be painful because relationships are connected to the heart and soul. Dare I say it? Emotional pain can be more severe than physical pain, and it is rarely more felt than when you have to say goodbye to someone you're invested in, and do it for the sake of your own healing.

The response of others to your healing process, or any endeavor to better yourself, falls into five categories. To put it a different way, the people around you can be identified in five ways. As I share them, names will start popping into your head and it'll click; you'll identify.

Spectators

Every single one of us has people in our lives that are not necessarily in our inner circle, but they're looking on. They're watching us. They're spectators. A spectator's general opinion is, "I see what you're doing, and it really doesn't make sense to me." There are many times when I have done something, in obedience to the Lord, and it didn't make any sense to me. How could it make sense to other people? Spectators will just stand back and watch. What you're doing doesn't really mean anything to them. They don't even necessarily want to be associated with you; they just want to be spectators. Spectators may think, "I'm going to watch you fail. I'm going to watch you trip. I'm going to watch you mess up. I'm going to watch you get disappointed." Spectators can be negative by nature. They are the general public who feed on drama and, sometimes, the misfortune of others.

Spectators want to see the outcome. They just want to be entertained.

Supporters

Supporters are also not necessarily in your circle, but they're acquaintances. They know and love you from a distance and generally support what you are doing. They're not always plugged into your life, but they want you to win, they want you to succeed, and they want you to be whole and well. A supporter may think, "What you're doing is brave and adventurous, and I'm rooting for you." They are usually on the fringe—the outer circle—but they keep up with you.

Supporters like social media. They can watch you online. They may or may not engage you in conversation, but they consider you a "friend." These are the people that admire you for what you're doing but rarely communicate that sentiment. Supporters hope you succeed.

Dissenters

Dissenters are people that don't have any faith in you. A dissenter's opinion is, "What you're doing is crazy. I don't believe in what you're doing. I can't believe you're doing this. I can't believe you're moving in this direction. I can't believe you're saying those things. I can't believe you're making those decisions." I'm not talking about reactions to impulsive, irresponsible decisions. I'm talking about your decisions to obey the Lord, to move toward health, to pull away from average, and to become extraordinary. Dissenters don't have the discernment to tell the difference. If they did, they'd be busy maturing instead of throwing rocks at you for doing so.

Dissenters can be people that were once in your circle but fell out with you over something. Anything. You're no longer in their good graces. You could solve world hunger and they wouldn't support it. Dissenters hope you fail.

Opposers

An opposer is worse than a dissenter. An opposer has empty hands and malicious intent. An opposer says, "What you are doing must be stopped." These are the people who will actively work against you. They will do everything in their power to stop you from accomplishing your mission and will recruit others to help them in doing so. These are poster children for modern cancel culture. They can't just disagree with you; they have to cancel you, take away your platform, and damage your influence.

They are usually manipulative people who practice undue influence on anyone who will listen. They've never liked you and don't mind saying so. To be honest, they probably don't like anyone in general. They will lie, cheat, twist your words, and paint an ugly picture to get people to turn against you. I call them "Absaloms." Absalom was King David's son who committed mutiny against his father in 2 Samuel chapter 15. Read the story some time. It has every turn of a soap opera: greed, betrayal, sex, murder, etc. Spoiler alert. Absalom didn't make it.

Opposers are convinced that you have to fail.

Passengers

Passengers are your people; your squad. Passengers say, "I'm on board with what you're doing." They don't even have to understand you. They don't question your motives. They don't have to have constant interaction with you. They're not going anywhere. Your passengers are with you! They want to be part of the outcome. They're invested.

You will eventually have to decide which group(s) of people you are willing to spend your time with. You don't have time to address every dissension or opposition to your future. Not everyone is entitled to get an answer from you. Those who oppose you certainly don't deserve the dignity of a response. You are the only person who can block out the noise.

Who's Counting on You?

"Faster than a speeding bullet, more powerful than a locomotive, able to leap tall buildings in a single bound. It's a bird! It's a plane! It's..." Go ahead, finish the line. This introduction from the *Adventures of Superman* television series (1952-1958) became infamous in every household in America.

The line came to mind one day as I was out in the backyard looking up at a clear blue sky. I was just staring at it, having a moment, mesmerized by its vastness and beauty. Suddenly a bird caught my eye as it came into my field of view. It was so high that, when I looked away, I wasn't able to find it again in the bright blue canvas.

As I searched the sky for the bird, my eyes finally caught movement. I stared at the object for a minute, realizing it wasn't a bird but a commercial jet. I watched it soar through the atmosphere until it was out of sight. My moment of reflection turned into an epiphany.

From the ground, the bird and the plane looked the same size. They also appeared to be traveling at a similar speed. The altitude is what made the difference. While the bird was flying hundreds of feet high, the plane was flying thousands of feet high. The bird was flying between nineteen and thirty-seven miles per hour, but the plane was flying between 420 and 630 miles per hour.

The bird was flying in its own strength. The plane was being propelled by jet fuel. The bird was traveling alone, but the plane was carrying passengers. The bird can go where it wills and land anywhere it chooses, but the plane was on a schedule and had a specific destination. The plane can only land when the runway is wide enough and long enough to accommodate its size.

I could go on about the differences between the bird and plane that I saw, but from the ground, you can't see any of those differences. In fact, if the two were to pass through my field of view at precisely the same time and position, the bird could even eclipse the plane from my vision. In this equation, my perspective is everything.

What is your perspective? Do you have goals and dreams? Do you have purpose and destiny? Of course, you do. Can you articulate those things at this stage of your life? If you can't, don't be discouraged. It's never too late to define who and what you are.

I want you to answer a more specific question though. It's a question that forces you to consider your perspective. How big is your dream? If you're not sure what it is yet, how big do you want your dream to be? Do you want your dream to be like the bird? Do you want to travel from point A to point B and just enjoy the journey? Do you want to go through life in your own power, at your own pace, moving with the wind and landing wherever you will? I suppose there's nothing wrong with that.

What if I told you your dream can be like the jet. You can fly higher, go faster, cover more ground, reach many destinations and live an intentional, empowered life, and take passengers. It all depends upon your perspective.

From my view on the ground, I don't see the atmosphere in which the plane has to fly. I don't feel the extreme conditions through which the plane has to fly. From my view, it looks like a smooth and level flight, but I don't feel the turbulence. I'm not at the controls fighting the elevation. I'm not looking at the instruments and gauges. From the pilot's perspective, the plane might be bouncing up and down. He might see the storm that is up ahead. The pilot isn't just responsible for the plane but also the passengers.

The air traffic controller's perspective is different from mine. He's looking at a larger picture. He sees the plane, the destination, the path that needs to be taken to keep from colliding with other planes, and the speed and altitude that must be traveled to reach the destination at the appointed time. He sees the storms, he sees what's up ahead, and he knows the terrain below. He has the flight plan.

If I were to be looking up into the sky on a cloudy day, I may have a harder time seeing an airplane. The pilot will climb to an altitude that is above those clouds. I know this because I've been a passenger on those jets. There are times when I would look out the window and I couldn't see anything because we were ascending through these clouds. Then, when the pilot reached his cruising altitude above the clouds, I would look out the window and see the most beautiful sight: the top of the clouds. Those who have never flown have only seen the clouds from the ground. Those of us who fly have seen the clouds below us.

When God gives you a dream and a vision, it's almost never something you can do at the moment. It usually looks difficult, scary, and too far away to accomplish. It looks like an airplane from the ground. While I'm standing here in Cincinnati, Ohio, that plane I see up there may be going to Chicago, Denver, or anywhere in the world at 30,000 feet and roughly 600 miles per hour.

Isn't that how you feel when you look at someone else's success? They look so high, so happy, so blessed. Their life is smooth-sailing; they know what they want, and they are going after it. They can do anything they want. What I wouldn't give to be like them. If you use other's success to measure your potential you'll never get off the ground. That successful person you're comparing yourself to used to be standing on the ground looking up in the sky, just like you are. They used to watch the planes fly overhead and have dreams and visions of being that successful one day.

There are so many people that never got their dreams off the ground because of something that happened to them. Allowing pain and fear of pain to dictate your decisions will always keep your feet on the ground. How many aspiring entrepreneurs didn't launch that new business idea because the last one failed? How many people went through life and died lonely because they were hurt in the last relationship. How many athletes never played their sport again because they were injured in the last game. Fear of pain because of past pain is proof that you haven't healed.

When God gives you a dream, you will never be happy or fulfilled until you live that dream. God created you for that dream. You have to trust that He knows the end from the beginning. He wrote your flight plan. He knows the point of origin, the destination, the coordinates, the altitude, the clouds, the turbulence, and the storms, and He will get you there safely at the appointed time. The question is: Are you willing to get off the ground?

It's not just about you. You could be the catalyst for someone else's dream. What God wants to do in your life may be so big that it will require you to have others around you. Those are your passengers. Remember? They are the people I mentioned earlier that are with you. They have bought into your dream and are on board for the journey. Their journey to accomplishing their dreams and visions may begin with being a passenger in your destiny. Your passengers are depending on you to get your dream off the ground! You will take your passengers to a place perhaps they couldn't reach on their own. They have a connection, a divine appointment to make, but the Lord is using you to get them there. The time will come when their dreams will take them farther than you could go, but you inspired them to get their feet off the ground.

Do you see how important healing is to your life and those around you? You must heal! There is too much to do, too many places to go, and too many people to inspire for you to run from the healing process. Say this out loud: Hurt people hurt people, but healed people heal people. Get your feet off the ground and get busy flying!

Once you've flown above the clouds, you'll never be satisfied to look at them from the ground. Don't let pain be your excuse to ground yourself. I'm here to encourage and inspire you to get back in the air; get back to doing what you were created to do. Your family is depending on you. Your passengers are depending on you.

CHAPTER 10

Do You Want to See My Scar?

When I choose a new book to read, I ask myself a question: What makes the author an authority on this subject? If I'm reading a leadership book, I want to know that the author is a successful leader. If it's a personal finance book, I want to know that the author is successful financially. If I'm going to buy what someone is selling, I have to be confident it's credible. Otherwise, what value is added to my life by reading what they have to say?

What makes me an authority on emotional, spiritual, and mental healing? Not formal education, certification, or a license but experience. Anyone who has experienced personal brokenness and subsequent genuine healing has the credibility to speak with wisdom and authority on the subject. Pain is common but healing is not so common.

Healing is something that requires a spirit of perseverance—an "I can't quit" attitude, the drive to get up off the ground, brush yourself off, and keep moving forward. Someone who has put in the work to accomplished that, and is willing to talk about it, is worth listening to.

Have you ever seen social media ads touting the ability to teach someone how to become a public speaker in a few easy steps? Frankly, if someone doesn't have something compelling to say, it doesn't matter how talented an orator they are. Skill can be taught, but only experience lends information with inspiration. I've heard sought-after public speakers who had nothing to say. On the other hand, I've heard speakers whose presentations left much to be desired, but what they had to say was so compelling it moved me to action. You can tell when a speaker or author is buying what they're selling.

Honestly, I can't teach you how to heal in a few easy steps. What I *can* do is give you sound, reliable information, forged in the fire of personal experience that will inspire you to believe in yourself, refuse to give up, and embrace the process of healing. It's not for the faint of heart, but it is for those who are not ready to throw in the towel and just exist until the day of their funeral. It's difficult but doable. It creates some pain, but it also creates purpose. How do I know? Experience.

Your Scars Tell Your Story

Like you, I have scars that tell a story. A scar is a mark that is left only after an injury has healed. The scar replaces the open wound that used to exist. My life bears that mark; it's living proof of my healing. It says I'm not bleeding anymore. It says the sting of pain is gone. It says I can talk about it without reopening the wound. That mark is valuable—not just to me but to anyone I allow to see it. It's my badge of authority on the subject of healing.

For most, their story is never told because they're afraid to show their scars. If you have walked the healing process, you've earned the right to show your scars. They're most valuable when they're visible. The reason many people hide them is that they still struggle with the embarrassment and shame that was created by the wound that used to be there. Whether that wound was self-inflicted or the result of a number of other variables, the feeling of not being okay and the social pressure to mask it leaves one with the feeling there is something wrong with them, and everyone else is normal. This conclusion also comes from personal experience.

How do you view the scars of your heart? Are they marks of shame or do you see them as an opportunity to tell your story? Someone with a pronounced physical scar in a conspicuous place on their body might wear clothing to keep it hidden because they are self-conscious. A child doesn't do that. A child will show everyone who will look.

My little brother was a daredevil. He was the exact opposite of me: three years his senior and afraid of any and all forms of risk. I was a rule follower and proud to announce that my abundance of caution prevented me from ever breaking a bone or needing stitches. My baby brother, however, sustained enough injuries for two boys. One of the most memorable injuries was the result of a go-kart crash. It was a three-horsepower two-seater with a chain that spent more time off the gears than on. One sunny, hot, summer, mid-Ohio day, Ryan took off behind the wheel. I'm going to guess he was about eight or nine years old. He followed the worn path we had created around the yard, through a field, around our grandparents' yard up the street, then back down the sidewalk to our house. I watched in nervous anticipation, as I was sure my accident-prone sibling was not coming out of this unscathed.

Sure enough, he found the two-foot drop-off between Grandma's yard and the end of our dead-end street. We had jumped it several times with me behind the wheel, but I had never done what he did that day. Ryan managed to hit it just right (or wrong) and flip the go-kart over. Did I mention this three-horsepower hot rod had no roll cage? I saw this unfold from a distance and ran as fast as I could to the scene of the crash, assured of the almost certain tragedy of some kind. When I got to him, I heard him crying, flipped the go-kart off of him, and checked him for wounds, loss of limbs, that sort of thing. Fortunately, he only sustained some scrapes and one cut on his knee cap that would require a few stitches. Needless to say, I was a nervous wreck.

After the drama had subsided and the stitches were in place, Ryan was proud of that wound. He wanted everyone to see it and to hear the story of how he got it. He saw it as a battle wound, a badge of honor, a right of passage. He was a rough and tough typical boy and didn't let it slow him down. After the wound healed and the stitches had been removed, we were waiting for the school bus one morning and Ryan broke it open again while practicing his break dancing skills on the driveway. Off to the emergency room he went for more stitches.

If only we could be as transparent about our internal scars as my brother was about the one on his knee. If only we could overcome the discomfiture long enough to understand that allowing others to see our scars just might give them hope that they can recover also.

If pain is what's keeping you from being transparent, what you have is an open wound. You haven't completed the process that transforms a wound into a scar. Open wounds are more difficult to hide than scars. Open wounds bleed, swell, and are instinctively protected and favored. Open wounds hurt and the pain can be so severe that it overcomes your need to hide or mask the wound. Pain will make you speak without a filter. Pain will make you act out of character. Pain will make you desperate for relief. What you should understand about pain, though, is that its purpose is not to reveal weakness. Quite the contrary; pain reveals your strength.

Pain teaches you things about yourself that can't be learned any other way. You don't know what your threshold of survival is until pain has pushed you there. You don't know the depth of your commitment to something until pain has tested it. You don't really know your capacity for love until pain has challenged a relationship. Pain is powerful, but everyone has a limit.

Your wound should eventually heal. When healing comes, the pain should subside. Scars don't hurt. If your wound isn't healing, it's an indication that you haven't yet submitted to the process. You can't breakdance in the driveway when you just had stitches removed from your knee; it'll rip the wound open again before it has a chance to completely heal. Are you picking up what I'm laying down?

My scars give me credibility to teach you something about healing. The scripture doesn't just give us a promise of healing. It is very specific about the need for healing, the nature of healing, the process of healing, and most importantly, the purpose of healing. One of the things I love about Scripture is that it is relevant to where I am, what I'm going through, how I'm feeling, and what I'm thinking. God's Word is a living Word that penetrates the deepest recesses of our hearts and performs spiritual surgery.

When a doctor performs surgery to remove a cancerous tumor, it requires laser focus and meticulous detail to remove the cancer without harming the organ(s) to which it is attached. That's how God operates on our hearts. He doesn't just want to help us treat our pain. He wants to cut out the cancer and restore us.

CHAPTER 11

The Case for Healing

The Tree of Knowledge

Anxiety and depression began in the garden of Eden. God gave Adam and Eve a beautiful place to live. He gave them specific instructions that they could have anything they wanted from the garden except the fruit from the tree of the knowledge of good and evil.[97] You know the story. Eve was deceived by the serpent, she and Adam disobeyed God, and at that very moment, the human conscience was activated.

Until that moment man was one with God. God created man in his own image and breathed His spirit into man. Man enjoyed fellowship and communion with God. Man had no need for a conscience because he was not presented with the dilemma of distinguishing between good and evil. Fear had never entered the consciousness of man, and thus neither anxiety nor fear existed. It was a perfect, utopian world.

As the opening scene of creation played out, though, man's focus would shift from what he had to what he didn't have. The devil, in the form of a serpent, would challenge God's

Word, planting a seed of doubt in man's consciousness. Ultimately, man would believe the lie that contradicted everything he knew to be true, act upon that lie, and suffer the consequences of shame and fear, and for the very first time in human history, man would feel anxiety.

> *"The serpent was the shrewdest of all the wild animals the Lord God had made. One day he asked the woman, 'Did God really say you must not eat the fruit from any of the trees in the garden?' 'Of course we may eat fruit from the trees in the garden,' the woman replied. 'It's only the fruit from the tree in the middle of the garden that we are not allowed to eat. God said, "You must not eat it or even touch it; if you do, you will die."' 'You won't die!' The serpent replied to the woman. 'God knows that your eyes will be opened as soon as you eat it, and you will be like God, knowing both good and evil.' The woman was convinced. She saw that the tree was beautiful and its fruit looked delicious, and she wanted the wisdom it would give her. So she took some of the fruit and ate it. Then she gave some to her husband, who was with her, and he ate it, too. At that moment their eyes were opened, and they suddenly felt shame at their nakedness. So they sewed fig leaves together to cover themselves." (Genesis 3:1-7)*

A word study of the original text shows the word translated *ashamed* is "bosh." Oddly enough, it is also translated, "became anxious."[98]

In a nutshell, Man heard the lie, believed the lie, and acted on the lie, and the consequence was the birth of anxiety into the brain and the consciousness of man. So if this is, in fact, the origin of anxiety, then where does depression come from? That answer is found in scripture also:

> *"Anxiety in the heart of man causes depression, but a*

good word makes it glad." (Proverbs 12:25 NKJV)

Anxiety and depression are part of the curse that man brought upon himself in the garden. That's where it all began. Ever since men and women have had to bear its weight. The pattern is visible in the Bible. David said, "My guilt has overwhelmed me like a burden too heavy to bear" (Psalm 38:4 NIV). Elijah said, "I have had enough Lord. Take my life, I am not better than my ancestors" (1 Kings 19:4 NIV). Jonah said, "Now O Lord, take away my life, for it is better for me to die than to live" (Jonah 4:3 NIV). Job said, "I have no peace, no quietness, I have no rest, but only turmoil" (Job 3:26 NIV). Jeremiah said, "Why did I ever come out of the womb to see trouble and sorrow and to end my days in shame?" (Jeremiah 20:18 NIV). These are all people who were ultimately used by God and successful in life, yet they still bore the burden of the curse.[99]

Man as body, mind (soul), and spirit was separated from God because of the curse. God physically put Adam and Eve out of the garden of Eden; their minds were separated from the mind of God and their spirits were separated from God's spirit. Our separation from our Creator is the root cause of anxiety and depression and all other sickness and disease. Fortunately, that wasn't the end of the story.

The Tree of Reconciliation

The Creator, not willing to altogether abandon his creation, came to earth in the flesh of Jesus Christ to claim His creation again to Himself. The Scripture refers to Jesus as the second Adam[100] in that He corrected what the first man Adam messed up.

Jesus' death on the cross (the tree of reconciliation) was the event that reconciled the mind and spirit of man with the mind and spirit of God, that had been separated in the garden.

"And all of this is a gift from God, who brought us back to himself through Christ." (2 Corinthians 5:18)

This is why we don't have to settle for a life filled with anxiety and depression. Jesus has reconciled us back to God, opening up the path to healing, body, mind, and spirit! One rendering of *reconciled* as an adjective is "no longer feeling distressed or anxious."[101] We can now have the mind of God[102] and be filled with the Spirit of God.[103] We can heal from this mindemic.

There are many books out there dealing with stress, anxiety, and depression. Some are written from a mental health or medical perspective. Some are written from a psychological perspective, and yet others are written from a religious and spiritual perspective, each giving you advice on how to beat this battle going on in your mind. After investigating this crisis from every angle, I've come to the conclusion that healing from intangible pain is only possible by treating it from every perspective. If you only seek medical attention, you will only treat the brain but ignore the mind and spirit. If you seek psychological care, you will treat the conscious mind but neglect to care for the brain and spirit. Finally, treating your pain from a spiritual perspective only will leave your mind and body untreated. All three of these options by themselves are only throwing buckets of water on an inferno. We are body, mind, and spirit and, therefore, must seek healing for body, mind, and spirit.

The Unfruitful Tree

Healing from this mindemic is about cursing the fig tree. Let me explain what I mean. In Matthew's Gospel, chapter 21, Jesus is walking back to Jerusalem one day and comes upon a fig tree. He was hungry and decided he would eat from the tree. The fig tree had leaves on it, which meant it should also have fruit because the fruit always grew on the fig tree before the leaves sprouted. This tree, however, had no fruit on it. Jesus' response was to curse it. He said:

"May you never bear fruit again!" (Matthew 21:19)

Bible scholars have published several opinions as to why Jesus might've cursed this tree. I have a theory I've never read in a commentary. If the tree of the knowledge of good and evil in the garden of Eden was a fig tree, perhaps on that particular day, the fig tree Jesus saw reminded him of that tree. Perhaps Jesus remembered how Adam and Eve had been deceived by the serpent to eat from that tree and how Man had lived under the curse of it ever since. My theory is that Jesus cursed the tree because the tree cursed his people. Think about it. Man was cursed because of the tree; Jesus took the curse upon himself and nailed it back to the tree, and now He was cursing the tree as an example of the power He had given us to curse the tree.

I think of the unfruitful fig tree as a metaphor for unfruitful thoughts. These are the obsessive, evasive, stressful, worrisome thoughts that feed anxiety and depression. When you are hungry for love, joy, peace, and contentment, you have to find fruit. But anxiety and depression offer you the tree with no fruit on it and leave you just as empty and hungry as before. How do you break that cycle? How do you resist the unfruitful thoughts of anxiety and depression? You have to curse the fig tree.

This is how I learned to counter-attack the mindemic. When the obsessive thoughts of anxiety begin to interrupt my thinking, I refuse to dwell on them. I curse the fig tree. I even say it out loud, "Lord, I curse the fig tree." I don't give attention to and don't have time to wrestle with unfruitful thoughts. I curse the fig tree. Jesus became the curse on the tree of reconciliation so I could curse the tree of unfruitful thoughts. I challenge you to try it. It works.

Closing Arguments

Across the globe, hundreds of millions of people fight anxiety and depression. It is a leading cause of disability. Antidepressants are the second most prescribed drug for Americans, 73% of which have no mental health diagnosis. 800,000 people die by suicide every year globally. This is the mindemic that is destroying lives. It is no respecter of persons and affects the religious and non-religious alike. It is America's biggest crisis.

America's biggest crisis needs the God of America's founding fathers to intervene. Healing of a mindemic of global proportions cannot be bought, legislated, or mandated. It has to come through the Great Physician. He uses clergy persons, psychologists, physicians, and scientists. He gives us the knowledge, wisdom, and tools needed to overcome the challenges of intangible pain.

You can experience the healing you are so desperate for. Let God use a physician, a counselor, a pastor, or all three to bring healing to your body, mind, and spirit. Just as medical science cannot be ignored, neither can religion and spirituality be ignored. Science and faith are not at odds. They work together to bring healing to a hurting humanity. Whether you need medical treatment, a religious intervention, or the restoration of your hope in the framework of religious coping, take care of *you*. Do your part. Retrain your brain with God's Word.

Our Creator, God, is just as interested in our mental wellbeing as He is our physical wellbeing. Dr. Koenig worded it best. "The Apostle Paul talks about the 'fruit of the spirit' being 'love, joy, peace, forbearance, kindness, goodness, faithfulness, gentleness and self-control' (Galatians 5:22–23). These are the fruit of the spirit (the results of living a spiritual life). Most of the Christian scriptures are aimed at nourishing a distinctively religious 'spirit,' and their claim

is that doing so will produce the fruit of mental health."[104]

I want to challenge you to pray a specific prayer as a daily intervention to counter your anxiety and depression for the next 30 days. This prayer touches several aspects of your daily life and will help you challenge your pain on a daily basis. This is the prayer that I have prayed over my son and have challenged him to pray daily as well. I even call it "Seth's Prayer."

Medical science, the promises of Scripture, and our life experiences of answered prayer and miracles are all proof that prayer is effective. Pray this prayer; after 30 days, your stress, worry, anxiety, and depression will begin to give way to a peace that is beyond your ability to understand.

Seth's Prayer

Lord, I pray for strength

"The LORD is my strength and my shield; in him my heart trusts, and I am helped; my heart exults, and with my song I give thanks to him." (Psalm 28:7)

I pray for increased faith

"And Jesus answered them, "Truly, I say to you, if you have faith and do not doubt, you will not only do what has been done to the fig tree, but even if you say to this mountain, 'Be taken up and thrown into the sea,' it will happen." (Matthew 21:21)

I pray for peace

"And the peace of God, which surpasses all understanding, will guard your hearts and your minds in Christ Jesus." (Philippians 4:7)

I pray for work

"Whatever you do, work heartily, as for the Lord and not for men…" (Colossians 3:23-24)

I pray for encouragement

"May the God of hope fill you with all joy and peace in believing, so that by the power of the Holy Spirit you may abound in hope." (Romans 15:13)

I pray for freedom from fear

"Fear not, for I am with you; be not dismayed, for I am your God; I will strengthen you, I will help you, I will uphold you with my righteous right hand." (Isaiah 41:10)

I pray for health, mentally, emotionally, and physically
"Beloved, I pray that all may go well with you and that you may be in good health, as it goes well with your soul."
(3 John 1:2)

I pray for self-control

"A man without self-control is like a city broken into and left without walls." (Proverbs 25:28)

I pray for grace

"See to it that no one fails to obtain the grace of God; that no "root of bitterness" springs up and causes trouble, and by it many become defiled." (Hebrews 12:15)

I pray for confidence

"Therefore do not throw away your confidence, which has a great reward. For you have need of endurance, so that when you have done the will of God you may receive what is promised." (Hebrews 10:35-36)

I pray to recognize my purpose

"And we know that for those who love God all things work together for good, for those who are called according to his purpose." (Romans 8:28)

I pray you will meet my needs

"And my God will supply every need of yours according to his riches in glory in Christ Jesus." (Philippians 4:19)

I pray for influence

"For at one time you were darkness, but now you are light in the Lord. Walk as children of light." (Ephesians 5:8)

I pray for transformation

"Do not be conformed to this world, but be transformed by the renewal of your mind, that by testing you may discern what is the will of God, what is good and acceptable and perfect." (Romans 12:2)

I pray for rejuvenation

"But they who wait for the LORD shall renew their strength; they shall mount up with wings like eagles; they shall run and not be weary; they shall walk and not faint." (Isaiah 40:31)

I pray for a humble spirit

"When pride comes, then comes disgrace, but with the

humble is wisdom." (Proverbs 11:2)

Finally, pray these scriptures over your mind:

"Don't copy the behavior and customs of this world, but let God transform you into a new person by changing the way you think. Then you will learn to know God's will for you, which is good and pleasing and perfect." (Romans 12:2)

"And now, dear brothers and sisters, one final thing. Fix your thoughts on what is true, and honorable, and right, and pure, and lovely, and admirable. Think about things that are excellent and worthy of praise." (Philippians 4:8)

"Let the Spirit renew your thoughts and attitudes." (Ephesians 4:23)

"Think about the things of heaven, not the things of earth." (Colossians 3:2)

"We use God's mighty weapons, not worldly weapons, to knock down the strongholds of human reasoning and to destroy false arguments. 5 We destroy every proud obstacle that keeps people from knowing God. We capture their rebellious thoughts and teach them to obey Christ." (2 Corinthians 10:4-5)

"Don't worry about anything; instead, pray about everything. Tell God what you need, and thank him for all he has done. Then you will experience God's peace, which exceeds anything we can understand. His peace will guard your hearts and minds as you live in Christ Jesus." (Romans 4:6-7)

"So, letting your sinful nature control your mind leads to death. But letting the Spirit control your mind leads to life and peace." (Romans 8:6)

Bibliography

1   Ritchie, Hannah, and Max Roser. "Mental Health." Our World in Data, January 20, 2018. https://ourworldindata. org/mental-health.

2   Ibid.

3   Ibid.

4   Goodwin G. M. (2008). Major depression is sometimes described as the common cold of psychiatry. *Journal of psychopharmacology* (Oxford, England), 22 (7 Suppl), 3. https://doi. org/10.1177/0269881108094716

5   Jabr, Ferris. "Researchers Take a Closer Look at the Most Common and Powerful Triggers of Depression." *Scientific American*, February 7, 2013. https://www. scientificamerican.com/article/triggers-of-depression/.

6   James, Spencer L., Degu Abate, Kalkidan Hassen Abate, Solomon M Abay, Cristiana Abbafati, Nooshin Abbasi, Hedayat Abbastabar, et al. "Global, Regional, and National Incidence, Prevalence, and Years Lived with Disability for 354 Diseases and Injuries for 195 Countries and TERRITORIES, 1990–2017: A Systematic Analysis for the Global Burden of Disease STUDY 2017." The Lancet 392, no. 10159 (2018): 1789–1858. https://doi.

org/10.1016/s0140-6736(18)32279-7.

7 Paul E. Greenberg, Andree-Anne Fournier. "The Economic Burden of Adults With Major Depressive Disorder in the United States (2005 and 2010)." Psychiatrist. com, February 4, 2021. https://doi.org/10.4088/ JCP.14m09298.

8 Ibid.

9 Moore, Thomas J, and Donald R Mattison. "Adult Utilization of Psychiatric Drugs and Differences by Sex, Age, and Race." JAMA internal medicine. U.S. National Library of Medicine, February 1, 2017. https:// www. ncbi.nlm.nih.gov/pubmed/27942726.

10 Markets, Research and. "Global Antidepressants Market (2020 to 2030)- COVID-19 Implications and Growth." GlobeNewswire News Room. "GlobeNewswire", April 21, 2020. https://www.globenewswire.com/ news-release/2020/04/21/2019282/0/en/Global-Antidepressants-Market-2020-to-2030-COVID-19-Implications-and-Growth.html.

11 Sumant, Onkar, and Kavita Joshi. "Opioids Market Size, Share and Trends: Industry Growth, 2026." Allied Market Research. Accessed March 9, 2021. https://www. alliedmarketresearch.com/opioids-market.

12 "Nearly 7 in 10 Americans Take Prescription Drugs, Mayo Clinic, Olmsted Medical Center Find." Mayo Clinic. Mayo Foundation for Medical Education and Research. Accessed March 9, 2021. https://news- network. mayoclinic.org/discussion/nearly-7-in-10-americans-take-prescription-drugs-mayo-clinic-olmsted-medical-center-find/.

13 Nirmita Panchal, Rabah Kamal, and Feb 2021. "The

Implications of COVID-19 for Mental Health and Substance Use." KFF, February 10, 2021. https://www.kff. org/coronavirus-covid-19/issue-brief/the-implications-of-covid-19-for-mental-health-and-substance-use/.

14   Ibid.

15   Ng, K.H., Kemp, R. Understanding and reducing the fear of COVID-19. J. Zhejiang Univ. Sci. B 21, 752–754 (2020). https://doi. org/10.1631/jzus.B2000228

16   Steimer, Thierry. "The biology of fear- and anxiety-related behaviors." Dialogues in clinical neuroscience vol. 4,3 (2002): 231-49. doi:10.31887/DCNS.2002.4.3/tsteimer

17   "Coronavirus Disease (COVID-19) Situation Reports." World Health Organization. World Health Organization. Accessed March 9, 2021. https://www.who.int/ emergencies/diseases/novel-coronavirus-2019/situation-reports.

18   GBD 2017 Disease and Injury Incidence and Prevalence Collaborators. (2018). Global, regional, and national incidence, prevalence, and years lived with disability for 354 diseases and injuries for 195 countries and territories, 1990–2017: a systematic analysis for the Global Burden of Disease Study 2017. The Lancet. DOI.

19   Lee, Paul Yuh Feng, Amy Nixion, Amit Chandratreya, and Judith M Murray. "Synovial Plica Syndrome of the Knee: A Commonly Overlooked Cause of Anterior Knee Pain." Surgery journal (New York, N.Y.). Thieme Medical Publishers, February 15, 2017. https://www.ncbi.nlm. nih.gov/pmc/articles/PMC5553487/.

20   "Mind." Wikipedia. Wikimedia Foundation, February 15, 2021. https://en.wikipedia.org/wiki/Mind.

21   Hamer, Dean H. Essay. *In The God Gene: How Faith Is Hardwired into Our Genes*, 117. New York: Anchor Books, 2005.

22   Harris, Annaka. "Consciousness Isn't Self-Centered - Issue 82: Panpsychism." Nautilus, February 27, 2020. http://nautil.us/issue/82/panpsychism/consciousness-isnt-self_centered.

23   "Closer to Truth." Episode: What is Consciousness? PBS, n.d.

24   Mehta, Neeta. "Mind-body Dualism: A critique from a Health Perspective." Mens sana monographs vol. 9,1 (2011): 202-9. doi:10.4103/0973-1229.77436

25   "Closer to Truth." Episode. no. What is Consciousness? PBS, n.d.

26   Hamer, Dean H. Essay. *In The God Gene: How Faith Is Hardwired into Our Genes*, 117. New York: Anchor Books, 2005.

27   Minsky, Marvin L. "Why People Think Computers Can't." AI Magazine. Accessed March 10, 2021. https://doi.org/10.1609/aimag. v3i4.376.

28   Strobel, Lee. *The Case for a Creator: a Journalist Investigates Scientific Evidence That Points toward God.* Grand Rapids, MI: Zondervan/Willow, 2014.

29   Hamer, *The God Gene*, 117.

30   Leaf, Caroline. Essay. *In Cleaning up Your Mental Mess: 5 Simple, Scientifically Proven Steps to Reduce Anxiety, Stress, and Toxic Thinking*, 49. Grand Rapids, MI: Baker Books, a division of Baker Publishing Group, 2021.

31   Ibid., 70.

32   Diagnostic and Statistical Manual of Mental Disorders: DSM-5. Arlington, VA: American Psychiatric Association, 2017.

33   Kalin, Ned H. "The Critical Relationship Between Anxiety and Depression." American Journal of Psychiatry 177, no. 5 (2020): 365–67. https://doi.org/10.1176/appi.ajp.2020.20030305.

34   Zbozinek, Tomislav D et al. "Diagnostic overlap of generalized anxiety disorder and major depressive disorder in a primary care sample." Depression and anxiety vol. 29,12 (2012): 1065-71. doi:10.1002/ da.22026

35   "Anxiety Disorders: Types, Causes, Symptoms & Treatments." Cleveland Clinic. Accessed March 12, 2021. https://my.clevelandclinic.org/health/diseases/9536-anxiety-disorders.

36   "Depression." National Institute of Mental Health. U.S. Department of Health and Human Services. Accessed March 12, 2021. https://www.nimh.nih.gov/health/topics/depression/index.shtml.

37   Publishing, Harvard Health. "What Causes Depression?" Harvard Health. Accessed March 12, 2021. https://www.health.harvard.edu/mind-and-mood/what-causes-depression.

38   Alexander Kaltenboeck, Catherine Harmer. "The Neuroscience of Depressive Disorders: A Brief Review of the Past and Some Considerations about the Future - Alexander Kaltenboeck, Catherine Harmer, 2018." SAGE Journals. Accessed March 12, 2021. https://journals.sagepub.com/doi/10.1177/2398212818799269.

39   Strobel, *Case for a Creator*

40   Genesis 2:7, Job 32:8, 1 Thessalonians 5:23

41   Wallace, Wayne A. Dissertation. The Effect of Confirmation Bias in Criminal Investigative Decision Making. Dissertation, ProQuest LLC, 2015. https://scholarworks.waldenu.edu/cgi/viewcontent.cgi?article=1021&context=hodgkinson.

42   Saad, Marcelo; De Medeiros, Roberta; Mosini, Amanda C. 2017. "Are We Ready for a True Biopsychosocial–Spiritual Model? The Many Meanings of "Spiritual" " Medicines 4, no. 4: 79. https://doi.org/10.3390/ medicines4040079

43   Koenig, Harold G. "Religion, Spirituality, and Health: The Research and CLINICAL IMPLICATIONS." ISRN Psychiatry 2012 (2012): 1–33. https://doi.org/10.5402/2012/278730.

44   Koenig, Harold G. "Is Your Shrink Anti-Religion? Here's Why." Catholic Exchange, January 17, 2012. https://catholicexchange.com/is-your-shrink-anti-religion-heres-why.

45   Ibid.

46   Ibid.

47   Mueller, Paul S., David J. Plevak, and Teresa A. Rummans. "Religious Involvement, Spirituality, and Medicine: Implications for Clinical Practice." Mayo Clinic Proceedings 76, no. 12 (2001): 1225–35. https://doi.org/10.4065/76.12.1225. Italics mine.

48   Swinton, John. Essay. In Spirituality and Mental Health Care Rediscovering a 'Forgotten' Dimension, 112. London: J. Kingsley Publishers, 2001.

49   Ibid.

50   Charles R. Perakis, DO. "Soul Sickness: A Frequently Missed Diagnosis." Journal of the American Osteopathic Association 110, no. 6 (2010): 347–49. https://doi.org/10.1016/j.jada.2010.04.023.

51   Tobe EH. Soul Sickness: A Frequently Missed Diagnosis. J Am Osteopath Assoc 2010;110(10):609.

52   "What Is a DO?" American Osteopathic Association. Accessed March 19, 2021. https://osteopathic.org/what-is-osteopathic-medicine/what-is-a-do/.

53   "Reactive Depression (Situational) (Concept Id: C0011579) - MedGen - NCBI." National Center for Biotechnology Information. U.S. National Library of Medicine. Accessed March 20, 2021. https://www.ncbi.nlm.nih.gov/medgen/4227.

54   Mojtabai R, Olfson M. Proportion of antidepressants pre- scribed without a psychiatric diagnosis is growing. Health Aff (Mill- wood). 2011 Aug;30(8):1434-42. doi: 10.1377/hlthaff.2010.1024. PMID: 21821561.

55   Koenig, Harold G. Essay. *In Religion and Mental Health: Research and Clinical Applications*, 255. London: Elsevier, 2018.

56   Koenig, Harold G. Essay. I*n Religion and Mental Health: Research and Clinical Applications*. London: Elsevier, 2018.

57   Ibid.

58   Tolson, Chester L., and Harold G. Koenig. *The Healing Power of Prayer: The Surprising Connection between Prayer and Your Health*. Grand Rapids, MI: Baker Books, 2004.

59   Ibid.

60 Wang, David. "Crisis Intervention." StatPearls [Internet]. U.S. National Library of Medicine, July 2, 2020. https://www.ncbi.nlm.nih.gov/books/NBK559081/#article-105826.s7.

61 "Intervention." Wikipedia. Wikimedia Foundation, December 3, 2020. https://en.wikipedia.org/wiki/Intervention.

62 Koenig, *Religion*. 57.

63 Ibid, 255.

64 Ibid.

65 Ibid, 257.

66 Tolson, Koenig, *Healing*.

67 Boelens PA , Reeves RR , Replogle WH , Koenig HG . The effect of prayer on depression and anxiety: Maintenance of positive influence one year after prayer intervention. International Journal of Psychiatry and Medicine. 2012;43(1):85–98, Quoted in Koenig, Harold G., Religion and Mental Health: Research and Clinical Applications. London: Elsevier, 2018.

68 Byrd RC. Positive therapeutic effects of intercessory prayer in a coronary care unit population. South Med J. 1988 Jul;81(7):826-9.   doi:10.1097/00007611-198807000-00005. PMID: 3393937. Quoted in Hamer, Dean H. The God Gene: How Faith Is Hardwired into Our Genes, 179-80. New York, NY: Anchor Books, 2005.

69 Koenig, *Religion*, 258.

70 Newberg, Andrew B., and Mark Robert Waldman. *How God Changes Your Brain: Breakthrough Findings from a Leading Neuroscientist*. New York: Ballantine Books,

2010.

71   Gall TL . The role of religious resources for older adults coping with illness. The Journal of Pastoral Care and Counseling. 2003; 57: 211 – 224 . Quoted in Koenig, Harold G., Religion and Mental Health: Research and Clinical Applications. London: Elsevier, 2018.

72   Koenig, *Religion*, 186.

73   Wilt JA , Grubbs JB , Lindberg MJ , Exline JJ , Pargament KI. Anxiety predicts increases in struggles with religious/ spiritual doubt over two weeks, one month, and one year. International Journal for the Psychology of Religion. 2017;27(1):26–34. Quoted in Koenig, Harold G., Religion and Mental Health: Research and Clinical Applications. London: Elsevier, 2018.

74   Miller L , Wickramaratne P , Gameroff MJ , Sage M , Tenke CE , Weissman MM . Religiosity and major depression in adults at high risk: A ten-year prospective study. American Journal of Psychiatry. 2012; 169(1):89– 94. Quoted in Koenig, Harold G., Religion and Mental Health: Research and Clinical Applications. London: Elsevier, 2018.

75   Koenig HG . *Faith and mental health*. Philadelphia, PA: Templeton Foundation Press; 2005.

76   Ibid, 173-74.

77   Weaver AJ . Has there been a failure to prepare and support-based clergy in their role as front-line community mental health workers? A review. Journal of Pastoral Care. 1995; 49:129–149. Quoted in Koenig, Harold G., Religion and Mental Health: Research and Clinical Applications. London: Elsevier, 2018.

78   Koenig, *Religion*, 83.

79   Ibid, 53.

80   Ellison CG, Bradshaw M, Kuyel N, Marcum JP. Attachment to God, stressful life events, and changes in psychological distress. Review of Religious Research. 2012 ; 53 (4): 493–511. Quoted in Koenig, Harold G., Religion and Mental Health: Research and Clinical Applications. London: Elsevier, 2018.

81   Koenig, *Religion*, 274.

82   Interlinear Bible.

83   "Asclepius." Wikipedia. Wikimedia Foundation, March 14, 2021. https://en.wikipedia.org/wiki/Asclepius.

84   Ibid.

85   Dr. Eli Lizorkin-Eyzenberg. "The Pool of Bethesda as Greek Asclepion - Israel Study Center." Israel Bible Weekly, February 10, 2020. https://weekly.israelbiblecenter.com/was-bethesda-jewish-or-pagan/.

86   These are the self-limiting intrusive thoughts that must be abandoned to change the brain.

87   John Wilkinson, "The Case of the Bent Woman in Luke 13: 10- 17," Evangelical Quarterly 49.4 (Oct.-Dec. 1977): 195-205.

88   "Ankylosing Spondylitis." National Institute of Arthritis and Musculoskeletal and Skin Diseases. U.S. Department of Health and Human Services, January 14, 2021. https://www.niams.nih.gov/health-topics/ankylosing-spondylitis.

89   Judges 3:12ff

90   Ackerman, C. E., MSc. (2020, September 01). 12 Tips For Building Self-Confidence and Self-Belief. Retrieved December 18, 2020, from https://positivepsychology.com/self-confidence-self-belief/

91   Cherry, Kendra. "Common Defense Mechanisms People Use to Cope with Anxiety." Verywell Mind, February 15, 2021. https://www.verywellmind.com/defense-mechanisms-2795960.

92   Patel, J., & Patel, P. (2019). Consequences of repression of emotion: Physical health, mental health and general well being. International Journal of Psychotherapy Practice and Research, 1(3), 16–21.

93   Leaf, Mental Mess, 70.

94   Luke 13:14

95   John 5:10

96   William C. Shiel Jr., MD. (2018, December 27). Definition of ectomy. Retrieved December 18, 2020, from https://www.medicinenet.com/ectomy/definition.htm

97   Many theologians believe this was a fig tree.

98   Genesis 2:25, Interlinear Bible.

99   McDaniel, Debbie. "7 Bible Figures Who Struggled with Depression." Crosswalk.com. Salem Web Network, March 9, 2021. https://www.crosswalk.com/faith/spiritual-life/7-bible-figures-who-struggled-with- depression.html.

100   1 Corinthians 15:45

101   "What Is Another Word for Reconciled?: Reconciled Synonyms- WordHippo Thesaurus." WordHippo.

Accessed March 31, 2021. https://www.wordhippo.com/
what-is/another-word-for/reconciled.html#/C0-4.

102 1 Corinthians 2:6, Philippians 2:5

103 1 Corinthians 6:19

104 Koenig, *Religion*, 12.

About the Author

Jeff Wolf is an author and speaker based in Cincinnati, Ohio. He answered the call of ministry and began preaching at the age of 15. He is a graduate of Lee University and an alumnus of the Pentecostal Theological Seminary in Cleveland, Tennessee. He has served almost three decades in ministry and leadership as a national evangelist, lead pastor, and denominational leader. Jeff also served 20 years in the field of law enforcement, beginning as a police chaplain and eventually retiring as a patrol sergeant. He continues to serve his local police department as a volunteer chaplain.

Jeff is well known for his dynamic preaching style in local churches, camp meetings, and conferences. He is also an author and the founder and president of Resurgence, Inc., a non-profit organization committed to facilitating healing and restoration in the ministry community.

CPSIA information can be obtained
t www.ICGtesting.com
inted in the USA
HW042349070621
671LV00003B/136